Notes to a Software Team Leader

Growing Self Organizing Software Teams

Roy Osherove

Notes to a Software Team Leader

Growing Self Organizing Software Teams

Roy Osherove

This book is for sale at http://TeamLeadSkills.com

This version was published on 2013-09-19

ISBN 978-82-999332-0-9

Published by Team Agile Publishing. Yet another Roy Osherove "Project". More info at osherove.com

Tweet This Book!

Please help Roy Osherove by spreading the word about this book on Twitter!

The suggested tweet for this book is:

Just purchased "Notes to a Software Team Leader" on LeanPub. #teamleader

The suggested hashtag for this book is #teamleader.

Find out what other people are saying about the book by clicking on this link to search for this hashtag on Twitter:

https://twitter.com/search/#teamleader

Also By Roy Osherove

Beautiful Builds

To Tal, Itamar, Aviv and Ido. We have grown so much.

Contents

CONTENTS

Audio Book Available

This book is also available as an audio book:

- Professionally Narrated
- Over four hours of audio
- mp3 and itunes audio book formats

To get the audio book go to http://5whys.com/audio[1]

---

[1]http://5whys.com/audio

Acknowledgments

I'd like to thank Kevlin Henney for coming up with the idea for the title of this book.

You can reach him at http://www.curbralan.com/[2].

Thanks to Mandy Moore, Nermina Miller and especially to Linda Recktenwald for helping out with copy editing, spell checks and grammar.

I would also like to thank the early beta reviewers of this book, and especially Ofer Zelig, Leif Eric Fredheim, Mauricio Diazorlich and Eric Potter for providing many insightful and helpful ideas and corrections.

A big thank you belongs to the early purchasers of this book when it was still in its infancy at leanpub.com. They are the reason this book was actually finished.

---

[2]http://www.curbralan.com/

About Roy Osherove

You can always reach roy at Roy@osherove.com[3].

Roy Osherove is a senior consultant at ITVerket AS, Norway. He is the author of The Art Of Unit Testing[4] and this is his second book. He is also one of the original ALT.NET organizers. He consults and trains teams worldwide on the gentle art of unit testing, test-driven development and how to lead software teams. He frequently speaks at international conferences on these topics and others.

Roy has been leading teams in many roles for over 15 years, and has failed enough to write a book about it.

Other projects by Roy:

- 5whys.com[5] - The blog that inspired this book
- The Art of Unit Testing[6] - Roy's first book
- Osherove.com[7] - Roy's Personal Website
- Speaker Notes[8] - A blog for public speakers
- Beautiful Builds[9] - A book about Build Automation Patterns

---

[3] mailto://roy@osherove.com
[4] http://ArtOfUnitTesting.com
[5] http://5whys.com
[6] http://ArtOfUnitTesting.com
[7] http://osherove.com
[8] http://speakernotes.org/
[9] http://BeautifulBuilds.com

Roy teaches a course on **Test Driven Development** online at
http://TddCourse.osherove.com[10]

---

[10]http://TddCourse.osherove.com

Books Mentioned in This Book

The following books are mentioned in this book.

- Peopleware by Tom Demarco and Timothy Lister[11]
- Influencer: The Power to Change Anything[12]
- Management 3.0[13]
- Becoming a Technical Leader: An Organic Problem-Solving Approach[14]
- The Mythical Man-Month[15]
- Succeeding with Agile[16]
- Managing Teams Congruently[17]
- Managing Yourself and Others[18]

For more books go to http://5whys.com/recommended-books/[19]

---

[11] http://www.amazon.com/exec/obidos/ASIN/0932633439/?tag=iserializable-20

[12] http://www.amazon.com/exec/obidos/ASIN/007148499X/?tag=iserializable-20

[13] http://www.amazon.com/exec/obidos/ASIN/0321712471/?tag=iserializable-20

[14] http://www.amazon.com/exec/obidos/ASIN/0932633021/?tag=iserializable-20

[15] http://www.amazon.com/exec/obidos/ASIN/0201835959/?tag=iserializable-20

[16] http://www.amazon.com/exec/obidos/ASIN/0321579364/?tag=iserializable-20

[17] http://www.amazon.com/gp/product/B004OEINB6/ref=as_li_ss_tl?ie=UTF8&camp= 1789&creative=390957&creativeASIN=B004OEINB6&linkCode=as2&tag=iserializable-20

[18] http://www.amazon.com/gp/product/B004LGS53I/ref=as_li_ss_tl?ie=UTF8&camp= 1789&creative=390957&creativeASIN=B004LGS53I&linkCode=as2&tag=iserializable-20

[19] http://5whys.com/recommended-books/

Foreword

The career of a programmer is a complicated one. The early days or years are straightforward enough. You start as a junior, learning at the elbow of people more experienced than you. You make the mistakes everyone makes and come up with a few new ones of your own. Then you find your feet and gain confidence and experience, and you start to enjoy the feeling of just knowing how to solve this one, because it's just like the one you had on that other project. Over time you start helping the newbies, remembering what it was like to be one yourself. You achieve the heady heights of senior developer.

And then one day it happens. You end up in charge of a team. Maybe not as their manager but as their technical team leader. They look to you for technical guidance. Your job is as much about creating and sharing a consistent vision as it is about delivering great software. Personality clashes within the team are suddenly your problem. You have to mediate heated debates about curly bracket placement or whether tail recursion is better than iteration. Should we hack this into the legacy system or bite the bullet and do it properly in the new one? Becoming a software team leader is hard.

I'm really pleased Roy has written this book. It's all the advice I wish I'd had when I started leading software teams. As well drawing on as his own wealth of experience, Roy has invited contributions from people across the software delivery world, and the result is a companion and compendium you can dip into to find advice and direction, some of it contradictory, some of it counterintuitive, all of it valuable.

– Dan North, independent consultant and troublemaker. http://dannorth.net, @tastapod

Preface

There are no Experts. There is only us.

These two simple sentences always make me feel lonely. They were uttered by Jeremy D. Miller, a developer I had come to appreciate during my years in the software industry. Those sentences makes me feel like there is nobody else to turn to, that I have to start trusting my own instincts, and that whoever tells you they *are* an expert is either lying or wrong.

In my career, which is around 15 years in the IT business as of the time of this writing, I have come to realize that "There are no Experts. There is only us" is very true.

In one of my first jobs ever as a programmer, I remember joining a team working on a governmental project; The project was all in Visual Basic 6.0, by the way. The team, including my team leader, really had no idea what they were doing, and, because I *also* didn't know what I was doing, I *assumed* that whatever people were doing was the right way to do it.

As time went by, I started to read more books about how software development *could* work. I read books like *The Mythical Man-Month* by Fred Brooks and *PeopleWare* by Tom Demarco and Timothy Lister. I looked around and I could see all of the problems that those books were talking about right there in front of me, in flesh and blood. And I could also see a big silence.

Nobody around me seemed to say anything about the crap that we were building, the crap that we were taking from our managers and customers, and *certainly* nobody was saying *anything* about the crap we were giving to our customers and managers. Nobody was talking about careless, helpless programmers. It was all just *fine* for everybody. To paraphrase Louis C.K.:

Everything was crappy and nobody cared.

Now, these were *good people*. Some were my friends, and they did not intend to do any harm, for sure. They did their best, in the same way ants do their best to overcome raindrops along their path to the anthill. But they weren't looking *up*. They weren't trying to predict where from or *why* the rain falls and where to be more careful. They didn't plan better ways to get to the anthill, or to get better helmets for the rain (ok this analogy is breaking down).

They were just ... *there* doing their ant-like job. Project late? sure. That's life. Quality sucks? Sure. That's life. Debugging until 3AM? Sure, that's life.

Was I the only one reading books? No. Well, there weren't *many* trade books, but there were definitely quite a few. But the books they were reading were not getting them anywhere, and, if they could get them somewhere, they never seemed to find time to finish the books and get there.

There was no sense of craftsmanship. But there was also no sense of professionalism. There was just a big downward spiral for each new project, as far as the eye could see.

This workplace was not unique by any means. Many places seemed to be like this, in variations, along the years. I hate working at places like that. I always want to make a difference.

This book is about making a difference and getting other people to make a difference as well. It is the book for those who feel hopelessly trapped in their jobs, even though they are Architects, Scrum Masters, Team Leaders or Senior Developers.

This book will try to be the book I wish I had when I first became a team leader.

I Elastic Leadership

"The reasonable man adapts himself to the world: the unreasonable one persists in trying to adapt the world to himself. Therefore all progress depends on the unreasonable man." — George Bernard Shaw, Man and Superman

1 Striving toward a Team Leader Manifesto

This chapter outlines the principles for becoming and staying a good leader and also growing other leaders among your peers.

Leadership in general and team leadership in the software business in particular, where very little training, if any, is provided, are not easy things to accomplish or indeed to measure. We can begin with the knowledge that most people in software, like you, really have no idea what they are doing and what they should be looking at when leading their software teams. Yes, that was me too.

This book is written from my own personal experience of what worked for *me* in my time in the business and what *didn't* work for me when I was leading software teams.

I do know this: the way we work with our teams must improve. We must become better adjusted to the current reality and needs of our team, our business, and ourselves.

A few good years ago, I was speaking at a conference about programming. The person who introduced me also mentioned that I was looking for a job. So at the end of the talk, a woman came up to me and said, "We want to hire you as a developer." Boy was I proud of myself that day. I began working there, and the woman became my team leader.

My first job was to write some code that goes through various computers on the local network and searches for some specific things on remote hard drives (no, it was not a virus). I worked on it alone. As the day went on, I struggled and struggled. It was harder than I thought. Another day came and went, and I was still at it. My ego wouldn't let me ask for help. They had hired me off a conference stage because I was supposed to be an expert. How bad would I look if I said I didn't know how to solve this problem—the *first* problem I had been given at that job? No. I was determined to work on it until I had figured it out.

To add to my grief, there were no daily stand-ups, and every few days my team leader would pass by me and ask lightly how things were going. I would slowly say it was "in progress" and move on with a solemn face. A week went by and I began avoiding people's eyes in the hallways. I pretended to be busy and pensive, but I was drowning inside. Every day that went by, it became harder to admit I was stuck. Every day that went by, made it harder to ask for help; I would look more stupid with what little progress I had made during all of that time.

At some point, I took sick leave for a few days. I couldn't handle the silent pressure. When I came back from the leave, my team leader approached me and said, "Hey, by the way, that thing you were working on? One of the devs and I sat on it and made it work in a few hours." They had found a simple way out of my mess, and I felt both betrayed and foolish. I was fired from that company shortly after with a budget-cut excuse, but I knew better.

There were so many things that could have been done to prevent this Greek tragedy.

- I could have been a bit more courageous to say, "I don't

know," as soon as possible.

- We could have had daily stand-ups where my predicament would have been discovered early
- We could have set a rule whereby no one is allowed to work on something on their own for more than a day.
- My team leader could have approached me and done one-on-one meetings weekly or biweekly to discover what was up.

But nothing happened, until the worst happened.

The values I will introduce here, and throughout this book, can help prevent such events from transpiring or at least make them very unlikely. I hope that they can help spark a change in you, the reader, to become better.

1.1 Why should you care?

You might feel helpless in leading your team to do the things you believe to be "right." This book can help. You might feel like you just want to keep your head above water, and this book will help you accomplish much more than that. You might feel clueless as to what it is you're actually supposed to be doing with your (future) team. We'll tackle that too. You might just be broken and scared because you have no idea how you're going to get out of a bad situation at work. Welcome to the club. I hope I can help. I hope I can because I've been there—clueless and scared. I was lucky enough to have some good mentors along the way who challenged me to do the things that I was scared to do, to get out of my comfort zone, and to learn things I didn't even know that I didn't know.

I think team leaders around the world all suffer from some of the same basic bad experiences. Most of us weren't taught how to do this type of work, and most of us are never going to get mentors to help us through it. Maybe what we're all missing are some good old-fashioned people skills. Maybe we're missing some direction, some overall purpose for why we're taking on this role of leading others. I feel that if we go unarmed, without a sense of purpose and strategy, into a leadership role in software, we've already lost the battle to create real teams. Yes, our head might be just above water, but are we really there just to slog through another day? Are we supposed to be this helpless? We want to be leaders who create not only real value but also happy teams, both fulfilled and loyal.

1.2 Don't be afraid to become management

A lot of developers who just got promoted to or who were just offered the opportunity to become a team leader seem to be against going into management. I can understand some of the reasoning, but I don't accept it. You might be afraid that your time will be sucked up by meetings, that you won't have time to do the things you love the most (like coding), and that you might lose friendships with people you currently work with. And I agree that there's a basis for those fears. We've all seen (or been) that person who doesn't have time to do what they love, or fumbles a friendship because they've turned into a boss from hell, and so on.

> Management, done wrong, can make these fears manifest into reality. But management done *right*

negates them.

Management, done right, is a very tough job.

That's why you get paid more.

–Paraphrasing Jerry Weinberg, in his book *Managing teams congruently.*

We will return to this sentence later in this book.

You can make time for the things you care about.

A good leader will challenge the team and people around them to solve their own problems instead of solving everyone's problem for them. As people slowly learn to solve their own problems, your time frees up more and more to do the things you care more about and the things that matter more (sitting down with people, actually coding to keep in sync with what's going on in the team and the code, and more). Doing your job as a leader and asking people to accomplish tasks or to challenge people could indeed feel weird, but, in my experience, doing it can garner *more* respect for you, not less. Yes, some things will change, but change is inevitable. You might as well own and control how things change.

It also takes time to challenge people, time that most teams do not have in abundance. Making slack time so that you can grow the skills of your team will be necessary.

An opportunity to learn new, exciting things every day

Nothing beats gaining new skills. You and your team should always be getting better and going out of your comfort zone to learn new things. This is essential to what a team leader does. To grow your team, you need to experience personal growth and challenges so that you can then use those experiences and know what to expect from your team.

Experiment with human beings

Yes. I said it. You have a team and you can experiment with goals, constraints, and the different leadership styles described in the remainder of this book. It is one of the most enjoyable and interesting things I love about being a leader.

Be more than one thing

You're not just a developer; you're also a leader. You can change things that bother you and do things that you think are right. How many times have you said to yourself, "I wish I could change X?" As a leader you can do something about it. If you choose not to become a manager, you'll have much less influence. As my friend Jeremy Miller once said,

> "There are no experts. There is only us."

If you haven't read the preface to this book, I think that statement is spot on. Sometimes you must be the person who gets up and does something. You'll be surprised by how many people will follow you. Remember that 90% of success is stepping up to the plate.

Challenge yourself and your team

I've heard this basic idea expressed in a couple different ways:

- Do one thing every day that scares you. (Eleanor Roosevelt)
- Get rejected at least once a day (also known as "Rejection Therapy").

These ideas are powerful and a good way to make sure you are actually learning something. I believe that learning something truly new is neither easy nor simple. In fact, many times it's scary, annoying, or discouraging enough to make you want to give up halfway through the challenge. Leadership, done right, can be very difficult to learn. But, when you learn it, you will have grown so much you will be amazed. You won't be the same person you were before embarking on this journey.

When you read the following words:

Great Challenge

What comes to mind?
Depending on your state of mind, "great challenge" can be taken either gravely ("I am facing a great big challenge.") or enthusiastically ("Wow, great challenge!"). Choose the second option.

Having said that, the following section may present a great challenge to you..

1.3 The Team Leader Manifesto

This manifesto is continuously being developed and refined. You can find the latest version of it at http://5whys.com/manifesto.

For us as team leaders, the goal and the way we measure our work is the overall growth in skills of self-organization and self-maintenance in each member of our team and the team as a whole.

To that end:

- We accept that the team's needs from us change continuously based on their skills for handling the current reality of work, so we embrace a continuously changing leadership style over a one-style-fits-all leadership approach.
- We believe in challenging ourselves and our teams to always get better, so:
    - We create slack time for the team to learn and be challenged.
    - We embrace taking risks for our team over staying safe.
    - We embrace fear and discomfort while learning new skills over keeping people within their comfort zone.
    - We embrace experimentation as a constant practice over maintaining the status quo:
        * With people
        * With tools
        * With processes
        * With the environment

- We believe our core practice is leading people, not wielding machines, so:
    - We embrace spending more time with our team than in meetings.
    - We embrace treating software problems as people problems.
    - We learn people skills and communication techniques.

1.4 Next up

The most important thing you will need to know before you plan how to lead is the three team phases: survival mode, learning mode, and self-organization, which the next chapter discusses.

2 Elastic Leadership

This chapter is a quick guide to recognizing the three team phases and the leadership types that make the most sense for each phase.

First, let's clarify *why* we need to define these phases anyway. The reasons have to do with our overall goal as team leaders. What do *you* think your role is as a team leader? For a few years, I had to guess. Nobody told me and I had no one to learn from. Now I think I know.

> Before we go on, I want to clarify about my future usage of some wording. I'll be using the words *phase* and *mode* interchangeably throughout the book. As a short example of how I use them, in the *learning phase* you go into *learning mode*. *Phase* is where you think your team is; *mode* is how you react to which phase you are in. Think of it like the fight or flee instincts that we all have. When these instincts take over, we act a certain way. So you might say that when we recognize we are in the survival phase, we initiate our survival instinct or survival mode. Or if we recognize that we are operating in learning mode while our organization is operating in survival mode, we can say we are really in a survival phase and we should initiate survival mode behavior and instinct.

2.1 The role of the team leader

In the past, one of my biggest mistakes as a team leader was that I didn't recognize that my style of leadership was irrelevant to the needs of my team. I don't blame myself, of course :).

During my first time as a team leader, my idea of what a team leader should do was very different from what it is today. Back then, my idea of what a team leader should do was:

> A team leader should provide to their team everything the team needs and then get out of their way.

Boy, did I think I was stellar! When people needed something—working code, infrastructure, a faster machine, or just an answer to something—I was their guy. By my own definition back then, I was doing a great job.

Of course, doing a "great job" back then meant that I had very little time for myself and was mostly in meetings or coding all day. I didn't allow myself to take even a couple of days to go on a vacation and actually *be away*. I was always at work because people needed me. And it felt great to be needed.

Looking back, I could have done so much better as the team leader. That's because today I believe the role of a team leader is vastly different from simply solving problems and getting out of the way.

2.2 Growth through challenge

Here's what I believe my role is today:

A team leader grows the people on their team.

I believe this should be your first "compass" in determining your behavior as a lead. You may ask, "What about delivering value to the company?" I believe that delivering value flows naturally from that. If people grow, value delivery also grows because skills grow. More importantly, the attachment and commitment of people to want to do the right thing also grows. Loyalty grows.

One of my mentors, Eli Lopian, told me once:

> "People don't quit their jobs. They quit their managers."

I think that's a very true statement (at least for the several companies I've quit). By growing the people on your team as team players or valuable working individuals, you are generating internal value for them—not just for the company. True loyalty comes when you have everything to gain by sticking around and you realize it.

Challenge

More things logically follow if your guiding rule is to help grow people. To grow people at work means to help them acquire new skills. For them to acquire skills you must challenge them. Therefore, you have to stop solving all their problems for them and ask them to solve problems on their own (with your guidance, of course). If you solve problems for your team, the only person learning how to do new things is you.

You're the bottleneck

By solving your team's problems, you're being their bottleneck, and they'll find themselves unable to manage without
you. If you're sick for three days, can you leave your phone
turned off? Or are you constantly worried and logging into
the company's VPN to check and fix things that nobody else
on the team can do? If the team has to wait for you to be
available to solve problems, you're the bottleneck, and you'll
never have time to do the things that really matter most.

2.3 Crunch time and leadership styles

Many of you might say, "Well, that makes no sense. We're
in crunch time! The release is late, and now I'm supposed to
take what little time we have left to teach people new things?
I have enough on my plate as it is!" And you'd be right, of
course. It's not always a good idea to start challenging people.
Sometimes, challenges don't make sense.

Challenging people is *one* style of leadership. Let's talk about
two more:

- **Command and control** leadership
- **Facilitating** leadership

Why do we need to talk about the other styles? Because
this style of *challenging* to grow isn't always a good idea.
Sometimes, a more command and control style of leadership
is required, where a leader needs to make clear cut decisions
as in

"Yes, we're using source control, and no, we're not holding a meeting on whether we should or should not."

Command and control is *sometimes* a good idea because there are times when a team leader must be able to direct their team down a path where the team has very little ability to face the current reality, with no time to learn how to deal with the current circumstances (such as when fighting many fires).

The third leadership style, **facilitation**, can be described by many agile consultants as

"Just lock the team in a room, give them a goal, and get the hell out of their way."

Agile methodologies sometimes call this a "self-organizing" team.

Facilitation is also a good idea sometimes, because sometimes the team already knows how to do the work and how to solve their own problems, and a leader will just get in the way of getting the job done.

So, which one should you choose?

2.4 Which Leadership Style Should You Choose?

It seems like all of the above approaches—*command and control*, *growing*, and *facilitation*—are good styles at different points in time. Team leaders have succeeded by doing each, but many have failed with each of them as well. So when *does* it make sense to use each of these different leadership ideas? When are those times when, as a leader, you need to take charge and start making some hard decisions? And when are those times when using *Command and Control* leadership will hurt more than it helps? When should you just lock them up in a room and get out of their way because they know what they're doing?

Just to get your head straight, I'll recap that we're talking about three different leadership types that I've seen in the wild:

- Command and control leader
- Coaching leader
- Facilitating leader (self-organizing teams)

Time for a small confession. It's easier for me to start with an answer to the opposite question: >"When should I **not** use each leadership style?

Let's tackle each one specifically and see when it makes *no *sense to use it.

Command and control

We've all seen or have been this type of leader at some point. You tell people what to do. You are the "decider." You take one for the team, but you also have the team in your pocket in terms of hierarchy, decision making, and control over everyone's actions.

The command and control leader might also solve everyone's problem for them. I once had a team leader who, on the first day that I joined the team, set up my laptop while typing blazingly fast on the keyboard and not sharing with me anything he was doing. When I asked questions, he muttered something along the lines of "Don't concern yourself with this now. You have more important things to do." (read that sentence with a heavy russian accent for better effect.)

With a controlling leader, there is little room for people to learn, take sole ownership of anything, or take initiative that might go against the rules. And that's just the way things are.

> *This approach won't work if your team already knows what they're doing or if they expect to learn new things and be challenged to become better.*

Coach

The coach is also known as "the teacher" and is great at teaching new things to others. The opposite of the controlling leader, the coach is great at teaching others to make decisions while letting them make the wrong decisions as long as there is an important lesson to be learned.

Time is not an issue for a coach because time is meant for learning. It's like teaching your kid to put on their shoes and tie their shoelaces—it takes time, but it's an important skill, so you'd be making a mistake not taking the time to let your kid to go through this exercise on their own, cheering them from the sidelines.

> This approach won't work if you and your team don't have enough free time to actually practice

and do any learning. So if you're busy putting out
fires all day, and you're already behind schedule
anyway, you won't have time to also learn or
try new things like refactoring or test-driven
development.

Facilitator

The facilitator stays out of everyone's way. Whereas the coach
challenges people to stop and learn something, the facilitator
simply makes sure that the current environment, conditions,
goals, and constraints are such that they will drive the team
to get things done. The facilitator doesn't solve the team's
problems but instead relies on the team's existing skills to
solve their own problems.

> *This whole approach won't work if the team does
> not have sufficient skills to solve their own prob-
> lems (such as slow machines, talking to cus-
> tomers, and so on).*

Now that we've discussed when *not* to use each leadership
style, let's talk about when they *do* make sense.

2.5 Leadership Styles and Team
Phases

Each of these leadership types belongs in a different phase
of the team's needs. There are times when a team needs a
commander, times when it needs a coach, and times when it
needs a facilitator. What are those times? I call them *the three
team phases.*

A beta tester for the book commented that the word 'phase' gives him a bad vibe "due to bad memories on some very poorly managed, "waterfall-style" projects". I'm still not sure what to call these things myself. *States* might be better suited, but I am still debating this back and forth in my mind. If you have a better name for what we are about to talk about, just email me to roy at osherove.com with the subject "Naming Phases".

2.6 The three team phases

These phases are how I currently decide for myself which leadership type is required for the current team. The question "Which leadership type is right?" should be asked on a daily basis because teams can flow in and out of these phases based on many factors.

Survival phase (no time to learn)

"Survival" sounds dramatic and is as alarming as it sounds. It doesn't necessarily mean coffee-stained carpets and a sleepless staff.

> I define survival as your team not having enough time to learn.

In order to accomplish your goal as a leader (getting people to grow), you need to make time to learn, so your main strategy, or instinct during this phase is to *get the team out of the survival phase by creating slack time.* In order to slack time, you will most likely need to use a command and control style of leadership.

Learning phase (learning to solve your own problems)

You can tell you're in the learning phase:

> when your team has enough slack time to learn
> and experiment and you're actually using that
> slack time.

Slack time can be used for learning new skills, or removing some technical debt, or at best doing both at the same time, such as:

- Learning and slowly implementing test-driven development, with people who have no experience with it
- Enhancing or building a continuous integration cycle, with people who have no experience with it
- Enhancing test coverage, with people who have no experience with it
- Learning about and refactoring code, with people who have no experience with it

In short, use slack time to do anything, and tack on the phrase "with people who have no experience with it" at the end of the sentence.

Your main goal as a leader (in order to achieve your overall role of growing people) is *to grow the team to be self-organizing by teaching and challenging them to solve their own problems.*

In order to achieve that, you need to become more of a coaching style leader, with the occasional intervention of the controlling leader, for those cases when you don't have enough slack time to learn from a specific mistake.

Self-organizing phase (facilitate, experiment)

You can tell you're in the self-organizing phase

> If you can leave work for a few days without being afraid to turn off your cell phone and laptop. If you can do that, come back, and things are going well, your team is in the quite unique position of solving their own problems without needing you to help them through.

Your goal in the self-organizing phase is to keep things as they are by being a facilitator and keeping a close eye on the team's ability to handle the current reality; When the team's dynamics change, you can determine what leadership style you need to use next.

The self-organizing phase is also a lot of fun because this is the phase where you have the most time to experiment and try different approaches, constraints, and team goals that will grow you and your team even more.

This is the point where you have the most time to yourself to do the things that matter most. As a leader, you have a vision to drive for. If you're always keeping your head down, you can't look up and see if your team is going in the right direction.

From my personal experience, most of the teams I've seen are far from self-organizing. My belief (though I have little more than gut feeling and anecdotal experience) is that maybe 5% of software teams *in the world* are truly self-organizing and are capable of solving their own problems. Some 80% of the software teams out there are probably in survival mode. (How often were you part of a team that kept putting out fires and never had time to do "the right thing"? I thought so. Me too.)

So, how do you switch to a different phase?

2.7 When does a team move between phases?

It's important that you recognize when your team needs a new type of leadership, so you'll have to keep a close eye on the team's main assets. Any event that can shift the balance of the following team assets can easily cause the team to have different needs from you as a leader:

- Asset #1: The team's knowledge and skill to solve their own problems
- Asset #2: The team's amount of slack time

Here are a couple of examples of events that could trigger a team phase shift:

- Let's say you are bringing into the team new people who lack the skills to solve their own problems.

  You might be going into the *learning phase*. If they still have time to learn, then you are indeed in the learning mode. You can use this time to teach those problem-solving skills to the new team members. Better yet, you might take the opportunity to teach some of the more experienced folks on the team how to mentor the new team members to solve their own problems. That way everyone is challenged and growing, not just the new members.

- Let's say you or someone else is changing deadlines on known goals.

  This could possibly remove any slack time that the team is using to learn. *You might be in the survival phase.* Time to get out of there fast by removing some commitments and making more slack time available for learning!

2.8 Next up

This chapter was a quick walk-through to recognizing the three team phases and leadership types that make the most sense for each phase. In the next few chapters, I will be going through each of the team phases, diving deeply into the specific leadership styles and techniques that have helped me make sense of things in the past.

II The Survival Phase

The survival phase is, in my experience, the most common one that I see teams living through. In this part, we'll take a look at how to know you're in it and how to get out of it.

3 Survival mode

The survival phase, the phase where I think more teams are located these days, is what I define as "not having enough time to learn."

3.1 Are you in survival mode?

If your team is constantly chasing its own tail and putting out fires instead of having time to sit down and experiment, learn new things, and apply them in a manner that makes them stick, you don't have enough time to learn. Can you send your team to a unit-testing course for a few days? When they come back, how much extra time do you provide for your team to apply what they've learned in a slower pace of development? Twenty percent more? Not even close. As we'll discuss in this chapter, 20 percent is not even scratching the surface. In fact, two to three *hundred* percent more is the minimum you should strive for.

The comfortable zone

As chaotic as survival mode may sound, I think it's quite easy to stay in survival mode. In fact, as annoying as it may feel to always chase and put out fires, I'd say many people feel right at home and are very comfortable with such a role. Staying up late, fixing that build, fixing that late-night bug—being a hero of sorts.

For some, being in a state of constant survival and fixing up things that should have already been fixed is within their own little comfort zone. Within that zone they know how to operate and what others expect of them, and most importantly, they know how to succeed in this cruel world. In fact, they *excel* at working where others feel terror or want to just quit.

Survival mode is a warm and fuzzy place where only those who painfully learned how to handle things just right can tread without fear and walk between the drops. Always within a hair of failure, they magically come, tired and fuzzy eyed, out of the fog of war, saying, "It was tough, but I got it working." That warm and fuzzy feeling of knowing what should be done when the crap hits the fan is what helps perpetuate this.

But there is something even more problematic about survival mode. It perpetuates itself. When we are in survival mode, we tend to stay there and not even attempt to get out. It's a sort of addiction cycle.

The survival mode addiction

In addiction, we convince ourselves that the current course of action is the only one that can make us feel better and help us through the current situation.

For example, we are faced with a dilemma: fix a fire or refactor the code (improve the quality and maintainability of the code without changing its functionality) so the fire won't flare up again. What do we do?

We convince ourselves that putting out the fire now will let us rest a bit in the near future, so we fix what aches the most. The *next* time this dilemma occurs, though, we remember that the last time we had this dilemma we made a choice that made us feel better immediately. So we turn to that choice again.

This *addiction* cycle of repeating something that only drives us further into the abyss can only be broken by:

- Realizing that we are in such a cycle
- Finding the courage to break the cycle by taking a risk and removing some commitments

Next, you'll see what steps you can take to get out of survival mode.

3.2 Getting out of survival mode

To get out of survival mode, you have to worry about one thing: creating slack time as a standard in your work process. To do that, you will need to remove some commitments, and that's a risk that many team leaders are afraid to take. If you are also afraid, here is a sentence I read in Jerry Weinberg's book *Managing teams Congruently*:

> "If done well, management is a tough job, which is why the pay is premium. However, there will always be those managers who want to get paid for the hard parts of management work without actually doing them."

That, in so many words, is an important lesson to those of us who chose leadership as a path.

By creating slack time, you can start using it, and, by definition, you are no longer in the **survival phase**, but the **learning phase**, which is what the next chapter deals with.

How much slack time do you need?

The book *Slack: Getting Past Burnout, Busywork and the Myth of Total Efficiency* by Tom DeMarco talks about "learning time" being up to 10 times slower than normal *productive* time.

If you are learning test-driven development (TDD), for example, that could mean that for a month or two, your developers might be up to 10 times slower implementing the same number of features because they need to experience writing them in a whole-new test-driven way. It might not be that bad for other types of learning, but you must be prepared for large amounts of time that you will need to take away from other work.

If you can't accommodate for such learning, perhaps you're in survival mode.

3.3 Making slack time—required actions

How do you drag your team by the hair out of survival mode so that you can begin learning? You can start by understanding the mess you're currently in.

Find out your current commitments

Making slack time is about getting rid of some of the commitments you already have, so that you can fill up that time with valuable learning time. To know which commitments you want to let go of, you have to start by finding out what you're already committed to. One of the simplest ways to do that is by hanging up a task (dry erase) board on a wall. Put on that board three simple columns:

- A to-do column, which will contain Post-it notes of tasks that await action over the next month
- An in-progress column, which will contain Post-it notes with tasks currently in progress
- A done column, where Post-it notes that list completed tasks will be moved

Also, make a special area on the board for Post-It notes that you will be removing from the to-do and in-progress columns in favor of learning time.

Round up the team and ask each person what they are currently working on, even if it's not written anywhere. Make sure to put a Post-it note for that in the in-progress column. Go through the tasks for the next month with the team and make sure you didn't miss anything. When you're finished, you should have a clear (and often gloomy) picture of what's happening.

Find out your current risks

Now it's time to see what hidden things might be holding you back. One technique I recommend is called "future memory." Assemble the team and ask a simple question:

> "Imagine it is six months from now, and our project has failed completely. Why did it fail?"

If your team feels comfortable enough with you, be prepared to hear some things that might surprise you. If you don't hear anything surprising, this would be a good time to have private one-on-ones with each person on the team to see if there are things they would be more comfortable saying in private.

Make a personal list of any risks uncovered and, if you uncover any in-progress tasks that people are doing that haven't yet been documented (private pet projects for the CEO, marketing requests that aren't listed anywhere, etc.), add them to the in-progress part of your wall.

Plan a red line

Now that you know your current commitments as a team, it's time to plan a *red line*. That's the point in time when you plan to schedule learning time as part of the work. After the red line, you commit to make time for your team to learn. T

he red line can be a month from now or at the end of the next iteration. Anything more than a month into the future and the risk of losing focus on the current task may be lost or slowly degraded into apathy. Once you have a red line, you have a deadline. Your job is to clear enough fires before the red line so that when you hit the red line, you feel comfortable having learning time.

The only way you'll feel comfortable after the red line is if you remove some of your current commitments—the ones you wrote down on the wall just now. So before reaching the line, you make a dash to put out fires. Estimate how many fires you'll be able to put out until the red line comes. For whatever fires you can't put out before then, you will have to delay your commitment to achieve them on their current schedule.

Past the line, your schedule will include tasks, but fewer than usual. How many fewer? It depends. Learning time, the time where your team experiences new skills and applies them to its current work, can sometimes take up to 10 times as long as usual. So while in theory you should make up to 10 times more time for each task for a few months, you should realistically plan for at least 2 or 3 times more than normal.

Based on how things go, you should add more learning time by removing commitments or by adding more buffer time to the current commitments. In this case, the word *buffer* is not meant to denote the "time we might need but currently don't have." It signifies "time we need to do slow practice."

Initially, removing half of the tasks you have or essentially making tasks take double the time might seem crazy. But imagine a team learning TDD. In fact, maybe your team actually tried to learn that. Writing in a test-first manner, the same code can easily take three to five times longer to write than when not using TDD (this is only from my personal experience).

How do you remove commitments?

You remove commitments by letting whoever needs to know, know. Your boss. Your stakeholders. Everyone who should care. Here's what you do:

- You show them the list of current tasks in progress.
- You explain to them that many of the current tasks could have been avoided if the team had had enough time to learn and become more professional (give some concrete examples).

- You explain your outlook for the next few months, in terms of commitments.
- You explain the gains from this move: reinventing the team as a professional team that makes fewer mistakes and learns from its mistakes.

Before you decide that this type of action isn't for you, for so many reasons, here are some reasons why you should do it anyway.

3.4 Why slack?

It's easy to just let this whole thing go, to just keep up with the daily stuff you're used to. Why would you want to tackle even more hardship than you already are tackling on a daily basis? But adding the slack will make or break your efforts. If you don't succeed in getting more slack, you won't get more time to learn, and you won't be able to grow your team out of future survival modes and teach them the necessary skills to deal with the world they live in.

Remember why you're doing this

You're going to go through this whole ordeal so that you can become the team leader you wish you always were—someone who fights for the team's right to learn and to always improve. This isn't an easy task. In fact, it's quite hard because it involves a bit of risk. Not as much risk as you think, but still, it is a risk.

The risk of losing face to upper management

You could lose face by admitting that things aren't going so well. This might actually be a win according to some, since you'll be getting more respect. You can't be the only one who noticed things aren't going that great, right? Nevertheless, it's going to feel a bit scary and risky, but remember, that's what you get paid to do: make things better, in the most professional, clear, and transparent way. Losing face is part of the game, and any would-be leader should be prepared to face such tough situations.

The risk of failing

Yes, it's possible that things won't go as smoothly as you wish they would. It's possible that you may not put out *all* the fires you promised by the red-line date. But you will learn so much from this experience, and you will become better and fix things as you go (change the red line or remove more commitments).

This is what you are being paid to do

What is the job of the supervisor at a car repair shop? If you ask me, when I come to the shop, I pay them to fix my car in a relatively quick way that won't hurt my budget too much. But from their point of view? The lousy ones believe they just get paid to decide on the shift schedule. The good ones feel they get paid to have a great workforce that's always ready and able to service the cars in a way that makes the customers happy. They are paid to make sure everyone in the shop knows

what they are doing and how to handle any car that comes in
the door.

Your manager might say that you get paid to ship software—or
make your team ship software. In turn, for you, that means
that you need to do everything in your power to make your
team the best at delivering that software, dealing with any
needs that come up, and being able to solve problems in a
quick way, without having any bottlenecks.

Translated: you are being *paid* to make tough calls and
judgments to the best of your knowledge and ability so you
can achieve this. You are being *paid* to get your team to a
level where they do things professionally. You are being *paid*
to keep taking the team to the next level of performance
and professionalism, because that's what will allow them to
deliver the software that needs to be written.

On the surface, all this seems unrequested, but it is what's
needed to get what's actually requested—working software
that can deliver real value over time.

What happens if management tells you, "Thanks, but no
thanks. No need to grow our teams. Just write the damn
thing." My initial instinct on such reactions is to flee that
workplace and find another place where management does
want people to make the best of themselves.

But you don't have to leave, because this just might be a good
story that you can keep to yourself and keep trying a little
more slowly and a little more quietly to get more slack time.
A year from now, if all hope is still lost, perhaps it's time to
pack up and go. But try to show results first, by making slack
time in guerrilla maneuvers, and then show success patterns
to management when you have some numbers in your hands.

Realize that you are going to break your own patterns

Yes, I'm going to repeat myself now, but just because this is going to happen many times. It's going to be scary and annoyingly unfamiliar. You won't be sure what to do at each specific point, and you'll sometimes have to rely on your instincts and a bit on my advice.

Getting out of your comfort zone is, by definition, uncomfortable, but that's how you learn new skills. In his book *Becoming a Technical Leader*, Jerry Weinberg tells the story of how he plotted his scores in the game of pinball over time. The score seemed to be consistently going up over time, meaning that he was becoming better, but just before every large quick rise in points, there was a *down slope* in points. These happened when he discovered new, interesting facts about the game he was playing.

For example, he discovered that when you have more than a single ball at the same time in the game, you earn double the points for every hit in the game. When he discovered this, he started *aiming* to have more than a single ball in the game.

When he first began doing this, he was really bad at it. In fact, he was a worse player with that technique and scored *fewer* points than he used to get without using this technique. But as he got better at this technique, his total score went up way higher than his usual average score.

In short, he learned how to look at and play the game differently, and to do that, he had to let go of his "sure footing" and unlearn things he had learned. To get to the next stage and to become *much* better than you are, you have to let go of the things you already know. You have to let go of the safety of the current position you're in, so that you climb to the next level. The same applies to what you're about to do as a team leader. You're about to take a risk, do something you've never done before, and change circumstances that seem almost unchangeable. In the process, you will learn many new things that nobody said weren't scary.

Nobody said you won't fall down a few times while you learn a new skill. Eventually, you realize that in life you always have to get uncomfortable before you learn new skills, and that this is just a phase of learning—you'll learn to even *like* it a bit. When this happens to me—when I feel uncomfortable, annoyed, or scared—there is also *another* voice in the back of my mind that actually makes me smile a bit, telling me, "Ah, I must be learning something. Cool!" You are about to learn a lot. Hold on, and don't let go of the end goal: to always get better.

Do not fear confrontation

As you break your and your team's patterns, you might get into some arguments with the folks who don't like change or don't trust you. Be prepared for this to happen. Many people don't like change. It's OK to disagree, and it's more than OK to say, "Let's agree to disagree," unless it's your manager, of course. In that case, don't be afraid to say what you believe in and what you think. It's OK if they don't accept your position, but you need to try. If you don't try, you'll never know if they might actually agree with you.

Don't run scenarios in your head about how a conversation with someone might go. That is usually just an excuse not to have a face-to-face with that someone. Realize this and meet with that someone in person. Be calm and rational. Make sure you can live with whatever is being decided. If you can't, you should say so.

You should strive to achieve a *real change*, not pretend change. If you need 100 percent more time and you get 20 percent more time, that's something you cannot live with. You have to say so. You have to bet the farm on this. You have to be able to say, "This is the best way I know how to run this team. Let me do my job." You should be able to say, "This is how I work. If you know someone who can do this job better and get this team to be better, you should hire them."

Eventually, know that if these things aren't accepted and you don't get anything you can live with, you should try to find a place that will respect these things. I believe it's OK, and even expected, to move on based on your work values. Don't stay where you're not appreciated and where you cannot change things. Don't stay in a place that makes you feel miserable.

Commit to a place where you can live with how things are going or change how things are going so you can live with them. If you accept survival mode for the way it is, it's your fault just as much as it is everyone else's fault. Even more so yours, because it's *your* job to stop midway and raise the flag if something is wrong. It's your ethical responsibility to do so. It's your ethical responsibility *not* to tell yourself, "Well, I told them. Now it's on them," and then stay and do the same old thing. That's a copout. It's up to you to make something out of this role you've chosen to fulfill. Being a leader can, at the beginning, feel quite lonely, but it can also feel amazingly fulfilling to drive for a real change you believe in.

Don't despair in the face of nitpickers

You might come across some "good souls" who will, with a smile, let you know about all the different ways you could have done this, about all the things that you might want to consider before doing this. It's OK to listen, and it's OK not to accept advice. It's important that you stay in focus. Your focus is to get the team out of survival mode, to make time for your team to learn new things, to get the team to be better. You might need to be a bit more *command and control* in your actions.

3.5 Command and control leadership

When the ship is sinking, the captain doesn't call a meeting. The captain gives orders. T

o get out of survival mode, you need to save precious time—time you will need to put out the fires on your way to learning. During survival, your goal is also to prevent mistakes made by the team, if you can detect them, and save time by making decisions on topics that, if you have meetings about them, will take a long time to decide in a team manner.

Yes, this feels like it goes against most of the ideas of trusting your team and letting them self-organize, but it's likely that the team itself isn't ready for self-organization. Team members may lack the skill to solve their own problems when faced with issues outside their comfort zone.

One of the common ways to recognize such lack of skill to self-organize is that the team keeps expecting the team leader to

heir problems for them. They might have learned
om you or from their previous team leader, but,
animal that has been kept in a zoo, letting them
the jungle will likely get them frustrated and
o get through a maze of issues they're not used
h. It's very likely that letting them self-organize
ing the proper skills is partly the reason why
ival mode today.

d decisions

decides for some reason not to use source
zip file mechanism as source control, you
a choice for the benefit of the team—to use
proper source-control tooling (for me this translates to "avoid
ClearCase!").

There's simply no time to start debating such a decision. Now
is the time to get out of survival mode. There will be plenty of
time to decide and learn different configuration management
options later, in the learning phase.

Play to the team's strengths

Now also is the time to get every team member to do what
they do best, not to challenge them to do something they will
do slowly or hate to do. If someone is a DB expert, let them
handle the DB until you get out of survival mode. You don't
have the precious time to let them do anything they are not
100 percent productive in (unless you don't have anyone else).

Get rid of disturbances

If someone is a bad influence on the team, for example, always pessimistic, your responsibility to the team is to remove that problem.

A beta reviewer for the book asked: "It's not clear I'd know if someone was being a 'bad' influence simply by resisting changes, especially if they feel they have a valid point of view. How do I decide?"

If someone resists changes quietly, sitting with you, during a one on one conversation, they are not a bad influence. they are not influencing anyone since you are the only two people in the room.

If someone resists changes in a room full of developers, that might still not be a *bad influence* because having conflict and making developers speak up about things that bother them should we a welcome idea in teams.

But having someone question decisions in the middle of survival mode in front of the whole team can be a show stopper, or at least slow down the start of the transition towards learning mode. Now is not the time for too many questions. Too much doubt, especially in difficult times, can bring a whole team down, in my experience.

One way is to get that person into a one-on-one talk and explain that for now, until you're out of survival mode, no down-talk is acceptable and that there will be time to talk about improving things when you have learning time available.

Another way is to move that person into a separate room for the duration of that survival phase or have them work on a different project or team for the duration of the survival phase. It may seem harsh, but harsh times sometimes call for harsh measures.

I'll add a warning here: I'd try the one-on-one first, but I wouldn't waste too much time having many such talks with that same person. The amount of time and energy you put into making this person play well on the team is going to be pretty large. That is precious time and energy you will need to get the team out of survival mode. You will have plenty of time to work with that person on their team skills when you're in learning mode.

On a related note, there is always the noted "no downers" rule, in which you don't allow immature behavior within the team. Phrases like, "I knew it would never work," count as downers in this book.

3.6 During transformation you will likely need to...

Once you have a green light from management to add slack time and to begin growing out of survival mode, you might need to make several changes to the way you manage yourself and your team. I'm saying "might" because you may already be doing some of those things, not because I think these changes are optional.

..Need to start spending more time with the team

How much time? At least 50 percent of your time should be spent either in the team room or talking or working with one of the developers. Move your computer to the team room. Make that your base of operations. This will allow you to become a "bottleneck ninja"—you will be able to detect when someone is stuck or the team is stuck and help steer them away into more productive waters.

In survival mode, you need to make navigation corrections all the time, to make sure your vision of a learning team is realized. A stuck team cannot put out the fires and cannot move onto learning mode because they haven't made enough time for it. To clear up 50 percent of your time, you will need to remove yourself from meetings.

Find all the meetings where you feel you are contributing little or nothing at all and the ones where you are benefitting the least. Find meetings that you might benefit from being at only every other meeting and ones that you can let go of completely. Cancel them as part of your overall effort to be more with your team. Use the same lines of reasoning that you used when getting rid of commitments. Your team can't function and get out of survival mode without you at the helm.

To work through that "needy" problem, you will need to be there so your team won't get stuck; later on, when you have time to learn and teach, you can teach them to solve their own problems so they won't need you as much. But there has to be a time investment first. And it has to be you because you are the one who leads the team.

What if you are not a technical team leader? It's still vastly important that you be there, to see any team problems that come up and how your technical leader is solving them. You should be there to see if there are any people problems that you can solve in some way. You should also be there for the technical lead so that they never get stuck answering a question that has to do with the vision or direction the team is taking.

In other words, be there for your team. Show that your words are not empty. Show that you are there for them as much as you expect them to be there for the company. If you ask your team to work long hours, you should be the last to leave during survival mode. If you leave before they do, you will create, at some point, a silent mutiny where people don't work but appear to. Resentment is a powerful enemy. You should be there feeling their pain while getting out of survival mode. You should be there to set a personal example. If you want to get out early, tell them they can get out early too. But don't ask them for unreasonable tasks in that time. Be there for what *really* needs to be done and for however long it takes, until you get out of survival mode. If longer hours for a month are needed, you should be there.

Personally, I'm against longer hours because I feel they just generate tired employees who will break at crunch time or will just create more fires. But I'm OK with a couple of days longer than usual to solve something that has gone horribly wrong, as long as it's not the norm.

..Need to take ownership of your team

Your team may be taking tasks from multiple stakeholders. That's not a bad thing per se, but if your team is in survival mode, it might be that the team's lack of skill or technique in handling multiple stakeholder requests at the same time is one of the causes of survival mode. If a team member says "yes" to a task simply because they do not want to let down the requesting party, without regard for the current schedule and commitments, that's a cause for action.

One possible action could be to make the decision for the duration of the survival phase and until otherwise stated that you, the team leader, will be the only funnel through which the team will be taking tasks, and stakeholder conversations should take place through you. This can help make sure the team stays focused on fixing the current fires and also gives you the opportunity to react when conflicting requests come in and act accordingly.

For example, you could talk to the stakeholder and explain the current priority of the tasks. You could replace a current task with a stakeholder task. As long as you're in control of what the team does, you're able to direct the team out of survival phase. If you don't control your team, someone else will and probably already is.

Learn how to say no by saying yes

One way to refuse stakeholder requests is by letting the requesting party realize for themselves that there are better ways to spend the team's time. One of the best ways I know to accomplish that is by having the walled task board with Post-it notes of what's currently in progress and what's coming up, sorted by priority (most important tasks are closer to the top).

If your stakeholder wants feature X, bring them up to the wall and say "OK, which feature do you want to move down in order to build this?" Ask them to take down a feature from the in-progress column or the to-do column. This usually leads to an interesting conversation with the stakeholder about what each task means and how much time it was estimated for. By the end of the conversation, either the stakeholder realizes where the task fits in or you will. Either way, what wins is the value generated for the company.

..Need to start doing daily stand-up meetings

This technique is critical to get the team on the right mindset on a daily basis. Each day you have a team meeting that should last no longer than 10 to 15 minutes. In the meeting, each person goes through three basic questions:

- What did you do yesterday?
- What are you going to do today?
- Is there anything stopping you?

These questions are as much for the rest of the team as they are for you. Through the answers, you get to find out about team members who may be stuck working on the same task alone for more than a day or two and pair them up with someone.

You can also discover if people are working on the wrong thing or focusing their energy down a path that's not productive during the survival phase. The team gains important insight as to what's going on and what the main focus is. They don't work in their own bubble but, instead, they feel more like they're part of a larger effort. Having a daily stand-up meeting (yes, you actually stand up during the meeting, so it takes less time) helps you get rid of unneeded boring team meetings.

Before i get into the subject of code reviews in the next section, I want to discuss the notion of *a broken window,* because lack of code quality and *broken windows* go together hand in hand.

..Need to understand the notion of broken windows

A "broken window" is a line that can be crossed. It relates to "the broken window theory," which states that if people see an opening to do something, they will take advantage of it to eventually do whatever they want.

You can read more at this link[1] about this concept.

To summarize, the broken windows theory was first introduced by social scientists James Q. Wilson and George L. Kelling, in an article titled "Broken Windows," which appeared in the March 1982 edition of *The Atlantic Monthly*.

The title comes from the following example:

> "Consider a building with a few broken windows. If the windows are not repaired, the tendency is for vandals to break a few more windows. Eventually, they may even break into the building, and if it's unoccupied, perhaps become squatters or light fires inside. Or consider a sidewalk. Some litter accumulates. Soon, more litter accumulates. Eventually, people even start leaving bags of trash from take-out restaurants there or even break into cars."

So how do code reviews relate to broken windows? Turns out they a hotbed for broken windows.

---

[1]http://en.wikipedia.org/wiki/Broken_windows_theory

..Need to start doing serious code reviews

Code reviews are a great tool for teaching and learning, but during survival they can be used to mitigate a code-quality problem. As a team leader, if you realize there's a problem with the quality of the code that generates more fires than you're able to fix, it's time to do some serious code reviews. By serious, I mean full commitment to the task.

Here's what worked for me: *No piece of code gets checked in to source control without a code review.* Yes, even if it's one line of code. Even if it's not code, just an XML file, I still review it.

At the beginning, as a team leader, I would do the code reviews. It would slow down the team but the code quality became higher. Effective code reviews are *not* done via a tool or remotely—they are done when you're sitting side-by-side with the person or pair who just wrote the code. This personal way allows you to share and teach much more information than you can pass in a text-based tool. Don't skimp on this! If you're going to do code reviews because your code sucks, do them right. Otherwise, if you compromise on the quality of the code review, you create a "broken window".

If you decide that "some code" doesn't need to get reviewed, that's a broken window. Eventually people will move the line of what constitutes review-worthy code up and up until there's no line. By setting an "everything, no exceptions" policy, you help to make sure that there's no line to move up. Everything is included. During survival mode, that's important.

So far, so good. but what if your team is distributed? ### What if your team is very big?

If you have more than, say, seven people on your team (google for "Pizza Size Teams"), things become less easily manageable. It also makes code reviews much harder. In that case I would try to first break the team in to smaller teams, and then teach one person on every team how to review, and more importantly, how to *teach* the other people on their team how to review code.

If I can't break the team up, I would assemble a group of people (about one per five people) and ask them to be the code review gate watchers, and then would continuously sit with a different person of that team *while they review other people's code.* That could help me see where they can be better reviewers, coach them on missing technqiues, and scale up the code review process, without sacrificing communication and shared knowledge.

What if you are part of a "wide team"—a team that's distributed?

You might not have the option of having your leader sit with you, and that sucks. You have to use other means, like screen-sharing tools, voice software, and the like. I'm going to recommend a couple of tools for those situations, but know that this is never going to be as good as the real thing, and you should make it your goal to have at least some scheduled times where people come in and sit down with one another.

About tooling—at the risk of dating myself as soon as the book publishes—I use a combination of TeamViewer for screen sharing and Skype for audio in the background. TeamViewer is free and also allows giving the remote viewer the controls so they can actually code and change text in your local machine. This can be a bit laggy though, unless your Internet connection is amazing.

On Mac and Unix, and for vim lovers (the text editor you will love to hate and hate to love), use a combination of tmux and iTerm2 with vim over ssh, and be amazed at the world of wonder before you. For those who lived then, it feels like BBS all over again, but it works.

If you're not a technical manager, Google these terms, and get a better understanding of what you will want people to use to communicate more effectively.

3.7 Next Up

If you keep at it and live up to the principles outlined here, I'm sure you'll begin making time to learn. In the next chapter, I'll discuss what to do with this time and how to grow people to become self-reliant and self-organizing as a team.

III The Learning Phase

> "You have learnt something. That always feels at first as if you have lost something." — George Bernard Shaw, Major Barbara

This part discusses what happens when we're finally able to make enough slack time for learning and start using that slack time for learning new skills and growing our team to be more self-organized.

4 Learning to learn

I talked about this example shortly in the chapter about getting out of survival mode, but I plan to go a bit more deeply into it this time to show how learning works.

In his great book *Becoming a Technical Leader*, Jerry Weinberg describes how he visualized his progress in getting better at playing pinball. He plotted his points over time on a chart:

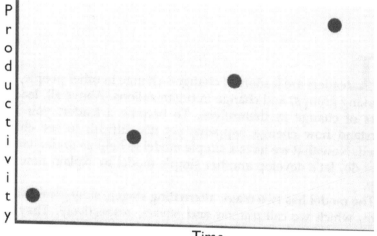

Learning rate

At first glance, it seems like there's steady progress—a steady learning curve in which he keeps getting better and better at playing pinball, but something interesting happens when you zoom into the chart. It turns out the progress isn't very steady at all:

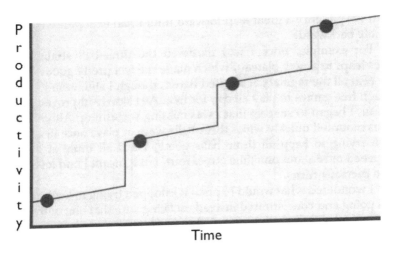

Learning rate zoomed in

In this image, you can see that there are two types of "progress":

- There are *plateaus* where the learning progress is slow and steady.
- There are *peaks* in which there's a lot of quick learning.

What happened at those peaks of learning? Those were the places where he discovered something new about how to play the game. Something that *changed* the game for him. In a way, it was a new paradigm about the game. For example, in one instance, he discovered that having more than a single ball in the game at the same time awarded double points for every original point. When he mastered the new paradigm, he became a much better player than he used to be, which accounts for the *peaking.*

As technical people, learning new things shouldn't be new to us. If you know more than a single programming language, you've already been through this peak. But there is a deeper meaning lurking in this story.

What happens when we show more points?

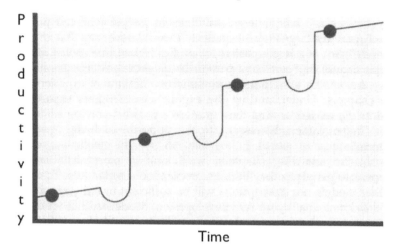

Time

Learning Rate With Ravines

Notice how just before every peak, there is a *ravine*? A drop in points/productivity/ability just before the big paradigm change? Those ravines are the adjustment phases.

> When you learn a new paradigm, you often have to "forget" some of the things you already know and learn how to do things very differently. In order to get to get to the other side, you have to let go of your sure footing.

When you learn a new programming language, you start out by being a much worse programmer than you are in the language you already know. Sometimes you can't even write a simple "hello world" program without a going through a dozen tutorials. You are much less productive learning a new paradigm such as a programming language than in the old one.

In time, you become faster and more productive, and soon you look back and realize you're now a much better programmer than you were, because you know two different languages, and you have seen various perspectives of the same ideas performed in different ways.

Our truest, richest learning comes from jumping into ravines, not by staying safely on a plateau. Ravines are everywhere in our lives, and they are the things that people usually refer to when they say, "What doesn't kill you makes you stronger."

Having kids is a perfect example of diving into a ravine. When my wife and I were newlyweds, we did lots of things together and were living it up. We used to travel a lot internationally and camp out twice a month. I remember complaining that there weren't enough hours in the day to do all the stuff I wanted to do. Then, we had a baby.

The baby ravine

Once our first son was born, we instantly became worse as human beings capable of managing themselves, their lives, and their time. We couldn't even manage our sleep and we were very very tired. Close family visited us almost on a daily basis to bring us food. We were too tired to cook, and I remember random naps in various places around the house based on where the baby fell asleep.

It was both an amazing time and a very difficult time for both of us. But a few months after our son's arrival, things started leveling out a bit. We learned to manage to sleep more, we started taking the baby out more, we learned to manage our sleep as a turn-based game, and we slowly made our way back into the normal-people territory.

A year into our first-time parenthood, we looked back at that time before having a child, and we couldn't believe just how much free time we had before that we didn't use. We had now managed to accomplish the same numbers of things we used to before his birth, only this time we had a full-time son. We were different people after this ravine, and we were *better* people in many ways. The hardship had taught us a lot.

For a while, we were doing just great. Then we had our second son. We instantly became worse as human beings, unable to manage our sleep routine and having to learn how to take care of two kids. For example, when we had just one child, we could take turns sleeping as the other parent watched him. Having two kids is a different story. Neither of us were able to stay alone with both kids at the same time because it was just too demanding and we were too tired. We had to figure out how to divide baby-watching and sleep routines, and we also had to remember to make food for the older child as well as a million other things that became more complicated with raising the second one.

A few months into having the second child, things started leveling out a bit. We figured out routines, and we also had the benefit of being less afraid and nervous for the second baby. When we were first-time parents, we were anxious about anything the he got close to. With the second child, we were more relaxed, because we realized that children are more resilient than we gave them credit for.

Six months after having the second baby, we looked back to the time when we had only one child, and we couldn't believe we had had such a hard time with just one. Having a single child now looked like taking a vacation, we felt. We were different parents than we were with just one baby. The hardship helped us learn many things, and we had grown immensely in both technique and spirit from this.

Then, in 2011, we had our *third* son. We are definitely more relaxed, but I was still unprepared for just how grueling things are with three kids. We are slowly learning to handle those crazy nights where we have a chain reaction of crying children and managing the alone time to spend with each kid. It's not easy, but we're happy.

I look back at having only two kids, and I can tell you this with a full heart, *having two kids is a piece of cake.* I can't believe we ever moaned and groaned about raising two kids. Even more so, I can't believe we ever had trouble with *just one child.* It's hard for me to process the fact that we couldn't even find, with a single child, the energy to make our own meals. We indeed are very different people and parents now, but we had to jump into each ravine before we could come out of it stronger.

> A beta reviewer for this book had this to say about my story about my kids: "Nitpickers may point out that as you adjust and adapt to your children, the children are also growing and adapting in ways that programming languages or tools don't when you use them, and that may have contributed to (but not been totally responsible for) your growth as a person. Nitpickers. Not me."

4.1 Embrace ravines

I think the true power of learning is to realize this simple fact: *ravines eventually end and you are left with new knowledge.* If you know this, you can start doing something incredible: you can begin plotting out future ravines that you might choose to fall into. You can plan your life as a series of learnings through ravines that you have carefully calculated to benefit you.

Becoming a team leader *could* be a great ravine for you, but only if you choose to jump in. Many team leaders keep the status quo and try not to touch or break anything. They never learn entirely new things. They never get an insanely better sense of the game they are currently playing; they just slowly grind away finding comfort in learning small things that make less of a difference.

How can you tell it's a ravine?

You might be facing a ravine if:

- You're scared to take this step because you might lose face, dignity, money, or friends.
- You feel like this isn't something that's meant for you.
- It will *change* you, how you perceive your world or your work or people you encounter(this is often hard to tell in advance).
- It will teach you new skills.

  Taking the team out of survival mode by removing commitments may be a big ravine for many team leaders. On the other hand, you might be fooling yourself that you're in a ravine when you're actually not, if:

good q: do we need to remove commitments (or not establish new ones) in order to get something done?

- You're not afraid to try this new thing.
- You feel there is no risk in trying out something.
- You feel that this is something you've kind of done before, just different.

For example, learning a new framework built into your favorite programming platform is not a ravine. It's fun, yes. But it's not risky, and you're not learning anything new about the game by learning a bunch of new APIs. You're just optimizing things locally.

A beta reviewer argued on the last point:

"If the framework were an Inversion of Control Container (Google it) and you wanted to start using it in your product, I think that making that change could indeed be a ravine. It's scary. You may break things. You're likely to kill productivity while people are learning how to configure and use the IOC. Et cetera."

I think there is some merit to that argument, but if it is a ravine, it's a very small one. It doesn't even scratch a real ravine's curves. It's not the vision I have in mind for you when I talk about learning new skills and getting out of your comfort zone.

Why? First, learning and implementing a new framework in your code is a perfectly safe endeavor. With source control, very little cannot be undone—even inflicting Inversion of Control frameworks on to unsuspecting code.

Second, it's part of a developer's job to use frameworks, and so it's not considered different or out of the ordinary to try a new one. Lord knows I've been through my share of people trying to use career-limiting frameworks at work, but no career has ever been limited by such a thing. It's simply taken by many as "Sigh! Another framework to work around."

The real scary part in the IOC framework suggestion is holding *other people* back, so it might be that the ravine one person might encounter is *working with other people* or *talking with other people*. That is a ravine indeed, because it's a skill that needs to be learned and practiced. And lord knows many people do *not* try this communication skill when implementing many of the frameworks developers are hammered with day in and day out.

If a developer came to me with that question, I would plan a ravine for them where they *had* to talk to people. Implementing an IOC framework might be the trigger for the real thing—communicating with others. But IOC is not the point. The framework is not the point.

Another example of not really learning: If you're a .NET programmer learning a new language on your home machine late at night after work, you're not really jumping into a ravine. Yes, it may be a valuable way to learn more things, but it's not a new skill.

A ravine might be joining a new team of people who *live and breath* the new language and it's associated culture, and will consider you a newbie, an intern, on that team. Immersing yourself in a new culture of ways of work is a ravine. Playing it safe is not. Yes, you might have a family to think of, but you should *plan* to get to work in that new culture of work, if you can. You should not plan to do things half-heartedly.

A ravine can also be a long-term goal ; I'd like to know math, because I was always afraid of that, and I know that when I conquer this fear I'll have a different view of my world of work and will have learned a new skill that opens many new options that I've always stayed away from. A ravine can be a short-term goal ; I'd like to confront someone who I'm afraid of talking to face-to-face.

The Intern

A few years ago I left a very confortable job as a CTO in a successful full .NET based company, to become an Intern at a small Ruby shop. I wanted to get into a ravine, and learn in the deepest way possible, what it means to be a Ruby developer, having come from a very different, Microsoft based, background. I wanted to know what I was really missing, or perhaps to know if it was all hype. It was a great choice. Everyone used a mac. I had never even touched a mac before. Everyone used the VIM text editor. I had only heard of VIM in my nightmares. Everyone was using Git source control. I had heard of it, but never used it in anger.

It was a difficult first few months for me. I felt like an idiot most of the time, but I learned things I never even knew I didn't know. Things that only being immersed in such a culture I could have "gotten". For example, I learned how to do very small code commits using Git. The culture of a small git commit is one I could never have learned form a Microsoft based company, because the way of work and way of thinking were so very different. I also learned the value of what I now lovingly call "Spartan Development". The idea that you use the lightest tools possible, zero to no debugger, and trust tests to guide your way. I would never have done that learning in the evenings on my own, because I would not *think* of doing it.

As an intern, I was forced to do things that were way out of my comfort zone, and thus learn things that will take with me for all future work. Hell, **I know VIM**. That is not something many developers can say. Knowing VIM, is like knowing regular expressions. You never know when you might need to use your skills, but when the time comes, you are ready.

4.2 Challenge your team into ravines

One thing I haven't mentioned yet is the concept of "homework." I'll expand on this in the chapter about growing people, in a couple of chapters, but a brief overview of this belongs here, since it's something you do at the learning phase.

Homework is actually something you do *at* work, or sometimes at home if you'd like. I call it homework because it doesn't relate to the day–to–day actual task, and it's not something that's officially designated as part of your job. It's usually a task that you incorporate into your actual work, such as "try to say 'yes' at least three times a day" or "be the last one to speak in every conversation."

Giving people on your team homework is a great way to teach new skills. It's important that this homework be a ravine-like task. If it's not scary or annoying to your team members, they might not be learning anything new. You can only ask someone to jump into a ravine with open eyes after you've done this yourself at least once. You need to be able to feel what it's like to be aware of this learning opportunity and to get over your personal fears and feel great afterward. Only then can you talk from your own point of view about the learning process.

You can inspire others to do jump into ravines only when you have your own story to share about some deep learning you've done and how it scared you. *Don't make one up.* If you want to learn something real as a team leader, learn to practice what you preach. Don't fake it—others will know, just like you've always been able to tell when someone was deceiving you. If you don't have a story, do something real, and only then share it.

You should, of course, explain this homework concept to your team. Usually, it's better if you do it in a one-on-one meeting because some people might feel more comfortable openly talking about their reservations from doing it without anyone else listening.

Sometimes, if the real learning is going to be a team effort (like moving the whole team to a new, more-challenging room), you should discuss the reasoning with the whole team as a group. And yes, it *will* be scary. Teaching a team how to jump and plan ravines is a ravine in its own right. It will feel awkward and unnatural, but it's part of your *own* learning.

Next Up

Next, we'll discuss another important technique, commitment language, and how it can help you and your team trust each other better.

5 Commitment Language

To understand how commitment language works, we need to talk about personal integrity. When we talk about practicing personal integrity, we:

1. Say we'll do it.
2. Mean what we say.
3. Do it (or we raise a red flag).

Creating a language of commitment is about getting people to actually say something and having them actually mean it. The first part is half-built into our conversations. We say we'll do stuff all the time, but we only half-mean it or we are only half-sure we can accomplish it most of the time.

Creating a language of commitment is one of the first steps to having team members who keep their promises to each other. Changing the way we speak to each other is important because the language we use every day leaves so many loopholes that help us feel like we said the right thing but still not feel like we're totally committed to it.

5.1 What does non-commitment sound like?

Have you noticed how you promise things to others? Look for usage of words that leave room to *not accomplish* something:

- "I hope to finish it this week."
- "Let's set up a meeting."
- "I'll fix these five bugs as soon as possible."
- "We should take care of that."
- "I need to lose weight."
- "I think I can do this today."
- "I'll try to do that as soon as possible."

A way out

Notice how all the above sentences offer us a way out? If we end up not accomplishing the thing we promised, we can always think to ourselves, "Well, I didn't say it would absolutely be done. I said it *might* be done."

Sometimes, we have good reasons not to commit fully, verbally to doing something, for example, if it's not totally up to us. The problem is that instead of telling someone, "I can't commit to that," we end up telling them what they want to hear.

Wishful speaking

This problem of *hiding* important information is very prevalent in our industry because we, the technical folk, like to believe in miracles. We also don't like confrontation. Telling someone what they *don't* want to hear is a form of confrontation. Why do that if we can just go about our happy lives, and things will somehow just work themselves out even if we don't finish what we promised? Heck, things are moving so quickly, it's possible no one will even remember what we promised we'd do.

And so this culture of wishful speaking continues and grows. People learn from each other how to make half-promises instead of real commitments.

5.2 What does commitment sound like?

I'm going to separate the idea of how commitment *sounds* from how commitment *feels*. Commitment *sounds* like someone stating a fact about them doing a specific thing, by a specific time or date. Here is the key sentence.

> I will [perform a certain action] by [a certain date].

The two basic building blocks of a sentence that has a commitment are:

- You *will* do something (not *might*, *should*, *want*, or any other inconclusive words). The word *will* is stating a fact.
- An expected end time or date. Without this part, the commitment is fully open to interpretation and is virtually meaningless. It has a big loophole: "I didn't say I'd do it this week, did I?"

Here are some examples of the previous sentences stated as commitments:

- "I will finish this by the end of this week."

- "I will send out a meeting invitation today."
- "I will fix these five bugs by the end of the week."
- "I will take care of that by Tuesday."
- "I will lose 1 kilo by the end of this month."
- "I will do this today."
- "I'll get that done by 18:00."

These sentences give you no way out. They make you sign a verbal contract with the listener, a contract that you'll feel at least mildly uncomfortable about breaking. This uncomfortable feeling about breaking this promise is the beginning of integrity, and it's also a good way to surface hidden issues.

5.3 Is it under your control?

By now, you may have strongly disagreed with one of the commitments I wrote in the previous section. If you haven't, take another look at the commitment sentences above. Is any one of them specifically bothering you? One of them should stand out like a sore thumb. Or at least it does to me.

If someone ever asked me to commit to something like this, "I will fix these five bugs by the end of the week," I would say, "I can't commit to that." Why? Because I can't really promise to fix a specific set of bugs by a specific date. Bugs, many times, are not as innocent and easy to fix as they may seem, so my commitment can easily be broken.

I call this kind of commitment, "committing to something that's not fully under your control" and it's the subject of the next section.

5.4 Commit to things under your *only* control

If my team leader expected me to commit to fix five bugs by the end of the week, I'd have a problem on my hands. How might someone react under such a type of pressure? Since your team members don't want to feel bad about themselves for breaking a promise, they'll do one of the following:

1. They'll *buffer* and commit to fixing those bugs at a much later time.
2. They'll say the commitment words but won't really mean them.
3. They'll say that they can't commit to that.

With behaviors #1 and #2, people don't mean what they say. With #1, it's entirely possible that they still might not fix those bugs by that end time. We all know some bugs take way longer to fix, since software is such a complex beast sometimes. With #2, they are just telling people what they want to hear, but internally they are telling themselves, "I'll play his silly commitment language game, but I know it will never work."

In both #1 and #2, people aren't displaying full integrity, because they *can't* be in full integrity about those things. We expect them to commit to things that aren't fully under their control. For commitment language to work, for *integrity* to exist, you have to *insist* that people commit only to things under their own control.

Let's see the difference.

5.5 Turn an impossible commitment into a possible one

If a team member commits to fixing bugs in a specific amount of time, as a team leader I'll ask them to change their commitment to something they can actually personally live up to something under their control.

What's under their control? Usually, their time and what they choose to work on are the only things under their administrative control. The trick is to notice someone's committing to something outside their control and then ask them to commit to *one or more steps* that can lead to this desired goal.

For example,

- "I will fix these bugs over the next week."

turns into:

- "I will work at least 5 hours each day for the next week to solve these bugs."

Here's another commitment that requires another person to accomplish. That person is not under their control, so it's impossible to commit to:

- "I will meet with David today, and together we'll decide how to solve this."

This turns into:

- "I will send out a meeting request to David today about solving this."

When people commit to things under their full control, they'll feel comfortable about committing to such a thing.

But what about the third behavior I mentioned (saying you can't commit to something)? When people have practiced the idea of integrity (discussed in the beginning of this chapter), they will feel comfortable saying that they cannot commit, and then you'll have discovered possible roadblocks that have never been mentioned before.

For example:

- "I can't commit to that because the CEO asked me to do another project, and I won't have time."
- "I can't commit to that because my machine isn't strong enough to crunch those numbers."

Now that you've discovered these hidden problems, you (or, better yet, your team members) can do something about them. For example, you can teach your team members how to solve that specific problem so that the next time it happens they won't need you to steer them in the right direction.

5.6 So how do you get them on board?

It's important to realize that it's not a "me" and "them" thing. It's a team issue, and you need to be part of the team. You need to learn and use commitment language as well.

Here are the steps I'd take to accomplish the language of commitment:

1. Assemble the team, teach them the language, and explain the whys.
2. Begin using this language in your meetings.
3. Fix just-in-time language errors.

Launch a commitment language initiative at a team meeting

Assemble the team in a single room, where possible. Explain that now that everyone has the time to start learning new things, you'd like everyone to start using a different mindset about promises and commitments. Explain that from that moment on, you'll be asking people to use concrete commitment language when promising to do something. Explain that you will be a bit of a pain in the neck over the next few weeks as you all adjust to this new way of speaking, and ask that people help each other out using the new language.

Teach the basics of the language (what words are non-commitments, what a commitment sounds and feels like) and see if you have several promises people have made in the past day or so that you can practice this on. If a pair promised the previous day to sit on something together, ask them to use commitment language to say the same promises in the form of commitments.

micromanaging bullshit [handwritten margin note]

Measure by feeling

See how using this new language affects how people make promises. Does it take them longer to decide if they can do something? Do they think twice before saying they'll do something? Do they dig deeper to understand what's really required?

How often do you personally get it wrong? Do people correct your language when you get it wrong, or do you have to catch it yourself? You have to set a good example here. The more people see you using this language, the more they will feel comfortable using it with each other.

It *will* feel awkward at first. It should because, when you learn new things and get out of your own comfort zone, it feels uncomfortable. It means you're learning something new.

Fix just-in-time errors

Remember to help everyone on the team fix their language, as it happens. The more you do it, the faster everyone will get used to it:

- "Would you mind using 'I will..by'' instead?" (and smile!)
- "So you will.." (and smile)
- "Great, you just forgot to use commitment langauge. Can you try?" (and smile)

Don't smile too much though. That will come off as creepy. I've been told.

Don't worry about feeling like a jerk, but be nice and polite. Leadership can sometimes feel pretty lonely even without being a jerk. Take comfort in knowing you're driving your team toward better integrity and that it takes a month or two to make a big difference.

5.7 What if they fail to meet their commitments?

If I set a meeting with you in a place downtown at 9 am, and on the way I realize I won't make it in time because of a traffic jam, I make sure to notify you as early as possible that I might be late. If I wait until the last minute that's just bad manners. For a project, waiting until the last minute to say something can be very destructive.

What happens when people realize they won't live up to their commitments, and it has everything to do with *integrity*. The basic idea is that they raise a red flag as quickly as possible.

Ask your team that as soon as someone realizes they will not make their commitment, they raise a flag as quickly as possible to the entire team or to you (if it was a personal commitment). The quicker they raise the flag, the bigger the chances that the team, as a team, can help out and increase the odds of that person's living up to their commitment.

5.8 Finishing the commitment conversation

When someone has made a commitment to you, and it's not clear, it's very useful to repeat what you *think* that person has committed to:

> "So, you can commit to working on this five hours, each day, for the next week?"

If the person says "yes," say, "thank you," and finish the current conversation. If the person corrects you, you've found out what they really committed or didn't commit to doing.

Always finish up with a thank-you because, from my experience, people don't know how to finish these conversations. A nice thank-you helps a lot to put a "dot" at the end of this conversation.

Can commitments drag on forever?

"My project manager will not like us not commiting to solve the bug, and just work on it instead. She will think we are just buffering."

That is one concern I have heard. But I have found that with some patience, it is easy to explain that some tasks cannot be proven to end by a specific time. Instead you can "cap" the maximium time you can "burn" on a specific commitment, and then regroup, replan, and recommit based on what you found. True agility.

5.9 Look for *by*, not *at*

One common gotcha that team leaders often make about commitment language is that they ask people to commit to a specific time of when something will take place. It's much better, safer, and more reassuring to ask people for an *end time* of when something will be done *by*, instead of an exact time.

Here's the bad version:

- "I will do this at 14:00 today."

Here's a better version:

- "I will do this by the end of the day."
- "I will do this by 15:00 today."

The difference is that you're not breaking your commitment if you still do that something, but it's earlier than when you promised. It also gives you some leeway as to when to accomplish the thing you promised.

Using by isn't always perfect, so when there are situations when stating a specific time makes more sense, judt use specific time, but those should, in my experience, happen much less often. Your first instinct should be "can we use 'by' here? no? nevermind."

5.10 Where to use this language

Use commitment language in daily stand-up meetings, in one-on-one meetings, and everywhere where promises are being made. I warn you that once you try this, you'll start seeing just how much non-commitment exists around you, among everyone you know and love.

This new skill you now have, of having a better understanding of the *conversational signs* people might show when not wanting to commit to something, will bring you both pleasure and pain. The pain will occur mostly when you need something from people and they use non-commitment phrasing, but you are not in a position to get them to change their language, and you need the most from them.

Take comfort that when those situations happen, you will have at least found out about a possible hidden landmine to achieve your goals much sooner than you normally would have. That gives you more options of what to do and where to save time, by not wasting it on non-commitment.

5.11 Next steps

Now that your team knows commitment language, you can start challenging them to learn new skills and ask them to commit to trying out different feats under their control, thereby learning new skills.

In the next chapters, we'll talk about growing people by challenging them and about integrity and how to use integrity meetings to measure the success of your team's self-organization efforts.

6 Growing People

In the previous chapter you learned about using commitment language. It's time to use it to grow the people in your team.

For your team to be able to self-organize and not need you, they need to learn how to solve their own problems. One of the simplest ways to do that is to stop solving people's problems for them and to ask them to start solving them on their own. This is called *delegation*, and it may feel awkward at first, but it's part of the idea of getting out of your comfort zone and learning new skills.

You *too* will have to learn a new skill here: to stop solving everyone's problems and begin mentoring and challenging them to solve their problems themselves.

Problem challenging Sooner or later a team member will come to you with a "wishful problem" such as:

- "We need faster computers."
- "I wish we had better communication with the customer."
- "We need to learn TDD."

When that happens, ask the person who said this one simple question:

"What are you going to do about it?"

Each word here is carefully selected:

"**What** are **you** going to **do** about it?"

This simple question, stated exactly like this, asks the person in front of you for an answer in the form of commitment language. Each word is carefully chosen to remove doubt that you are looking for anything else except commitment.

What if you ask it another way:

- "What do you think you *should* do about it?"
- "What *can* you do about it?"
- "How do you *intend* to solve it?"

All these questions evoke answers that have loopholes:

- I should do X. (Instead of "I will.")
- I can do X.
- I could do X.

As the person answers you, challenge them to use *commitment language*, as you saw in the previous chapter.

People may not get what you're asking them to say. They might keep answering in the same old ways. Remind them gently >"So you *will...*?"

It's not just simple delegation, though. It's about teaching people to solve their own problems, so it's more of a challenge for people. That's why I call this *problem challenging*.

6.1 How did I react the first time I got challenged?

I remember when my leader first asked me, "What are you going to do about it?" I remember a combination of thoughts and feelings:

- I felt angry because he asked me to do something that wasn't my job.
- I felt angry that he seemed to be lazying around asking others to do his work instead of doing what he was paid to do (to help me!).
- I felt betrayed a bit, because I came for help and found myself staring in the mirror instead.

Some of this bad vibe happened because nobody prepared me for what was about to come. The conversation went like this:

I answered: > "Well, I just came to you, didn't I? So that's what I'm doing about it."

I felt good about telling him off. He answered:

> "I want you to learn to do this on your own. It's a skill that you need to have if you are ever going to be a leader yourself."

That was a good answer. But who had time? > "I don't have time to do this (whatever it was. I don't remember). Can you give me more time?"

> "Yes."

I got more time, and I later also got asked to use "I will... by..." when committing to this new task.

It took me a couple of months, and some new skills, to realize that this was actually a great gift that I got, instead of a horse with no teeth. Don't expect it to be easy to have this conversation with your people.

6.2 When to use problem challenging

This technique comes in handy in several places:

- Day-to-day growth opportunities
- Daily stand-up meetings
- One-on-one meetings

Let's look at each one.

Day-to-day growth opportunities

As people come to you with a problem, you can ask them, "What are you going to do about it?" You can mentor them and give them ideas about how to solve their problems, but first see if they can come up with ideas of their own. Challenge them to solve it on their own, with you as their mentor but without your doing the work for them.

Daily stand-up meetings

As people come up with problems and hindrances in the daily stand-up meeting, challenge them and ask them, "What are you going to about it?" and see where it leads. Help them figure the problem out and don't solve it for them. Teach them to solve the problem on their own. Most importantly, teach them the thinking that led to the idea of how to solve it.

One-on-one meetings

If during one-on-ones, the team member raises an issue, see if you can help them solve it on their own. Help them figure it out, and mentor them to completion.

Next, let's talk about what happens when someone doesn't live up to their commitments.

6.3 Don't punish for lack of trying or lack of success

When people are challenged to solve their own problems, it's important not to punish people who didn't solve them. It's *their* problem, so they will continue to suffer for it. The consequence is that they will keep having the problem. If they care about it enough, they'll keep trying.

If you're not giving them the tools to solve it, though, that's an even bigger problem. You can't ask them to solve a problem and not support them when they attempt to solve it.

Having their back can mean many things. Here are the most important two:

- Give them enough time to work on the problem.
- Give them permission to approach people they need to without you.

Next, we'll take a look at a simple concept I used successfully many times, which I call *homework*.

6.4 Homework

Challenging for growth doesn't just have to be the technique to use when people approach you. You can add a more structured and planned growth trail for team members, by having bi-weekly one-on-one meetings where you can also discuss the idea of *homework*.

Homework is things that a team member could do better or things they *need* to do better because they hurt the team. It doesn't have to happen outside of work, but it may not be specifically related to the current work that person is doing (*sidework* might be a less-confusing name for some).

Things to consider as areas of growth during homework are:

- Something they feel will inspire them.
- Something that will get them out of their comfort zone (you can tell if they are afraid of doing it).
- Something that needs to change because it hurts the team (morale, productivity, teamwork).

Things that *don't* fit in, but seem like they do, are:

- Learning the latest buzzword technology on the same platform (I know technology X but want to learn this framework).
- Learning a new platform without learning its culture (I want to learn Ruby, but I won't assimilate with an experienced Ruby team).

You can usually easily tell the difference between a true growth opportunity and a fake one if you know what to look for:

- Absence of fear: If the team member is not even a little afraid of taking a step, it's probably not taking them out of their comfort zone.
  A good example of a true growth opportunity is switching to a different team or speaking to someone they are afraid to speak with.
- Absence of annoyance/frustration before starting: if the team member is not even a little frustrated or annoyed about how it's not their job to do X, you might not be truly teaching them something new.

  A good example of a true growth opportunity is doing work that was never part of their job description or sitting in a room with people they never had to work with.

In essence, homework is about learning a new *skill*, not a new technology. So always ask yourself and your team, what skills are missing?

Homework is a personal commitment, not a task

During one-on-ones, if someone takes on homework, they should treat it as a personal growth challenge, not as a work task. In other words, they shouldn't be punished for not doing it because they're the only ones hurt from it. The desire to get better and break your own limits is what drives this homework, not a manager telling someone what to do. That's why taking on a personal homework task should be said in commitment language but should be judged only at the personal growth and mentorship level, not at the work level.

Homework has follow-up

I consider it homework if I can get an email from a person at the end of each day or each week or have a one-on-one meeting each week about the progress they make. Any longer period of time and we start to lose focus or track of what's being accomplished.

Homework examples

Let's say one of your team members is a slow typist. In fact, they use the mouse for almost everything. This is hurting your team because people hesitate to pair with them because of how slow things get done.

You can sit down with this person and ask them if they knew they could become faster if they wanted to. Most devs would be thrilled at such an idea. You can then suggest ideas or, better, ask them for an idea of how to get better. For example, get a "blind typing" teaching program and measure words per minute over a few weeks.

Another example would be someone who's always negative. You know, the "it's never going to work" type you've had on the team for a while now.

The first step is to have a one-on-one with the person and explain that they can benefit much from choosing their battles. Homework here could be >"Say the word 'no' no more than three times a day."

Then, you can also ask the team member to email you at the end of each day when they said "yes" or "no" and why. This isn't about punishment; it's about being there as a mentor and personal reminder, someone to bounce ideas off and to give advice when needed.

Homework and its effects can take months to change behavior or craft new skills, so plan to give it three to six months. Don't expect results in a week for some things. Remember, one of the reasons you got out of chaos is so that you will have that extra time for people in your team to learn and experiment with new skills. Use that time and let people use it to try these new commitments. It's important not to overdo it, though, as you'll see next.

6.5 Pace yourself and your team

It's important not to push this too far. If your answer to every question is "What are you going to do about it?" you're going to stop getting questions at some point; It's going to be too quiet, and it won't quiet because people know how to solve their own problems. You'll see that they can't, but won't ask for help anymore. That's how you know you've gone too far with challenging them. So, make sure to challenge people on no more than a couple of fronts at the same time. Don't *swamp* people with challenges. Give them time to work on one or two challenges at a time and then move on to the next challenge.

Now that we are pacing ourselves, let's talk about when to step in even though people are learning.

6.6 Do you have enough learning time to make this mistake?

Sometimes you'll see people going down the wrong path on a problem and you'll have to make the decision whether you should let them follow that path and learn for themselves why it's wrong or keep them away from it completely.

That depends on how much time you can spare. If getting out of the hole they are digging will take longer than you've made a buffer time for, you might want to take charge and redirect the efforts.

Take, for example, having a team use no source control. If you lose all of your work, it would take too much time to restore. So usually you can't afford that decision.

That's why even if in the learning phase you should strive to be a mentor, sometimes you'll have to be a dictator.

6.7 Are there situations where you should not grow people?

What if you have a short-term consultant on your team? What if you're the team lead for just this project, and there will be a new team lead on the next project? Should you work on growing people even in those situations? My answer is an unequivocal "yes."

People who come across my path, even for a short time, will get the same amount of respect, expectations, and challenge from me as if they had been there forever. I try to always leave people whom I've led better off than they were, in terms of new skills and challenges. It's my personal integrity to do so.

If you conduct yourself this way, you'll find that people will want to work more with you and will remember you even years later, no matter how short the project was.

You never know when you're going to meet those people again, and you may find hidden treasures are lying in your future path just because a few years back you did the right thing with people who didn't expect you to. Show a personal example that even in the short term, you don't give up on quality (of people, of leadership).

6.8 Next steps

If all goes well, people should be getting better with new skills every week. You can ask yourself, on a weekly or daily basis, "Is my team better than it was last week?"

The next step is using what you learned to get them team

closer and closer to self-organization and measuring how close you're getting to that goal.

IV The Self-Organization Phase

"William: "I'm sure we can all pull together, sir."

Vetinari: "Oh, I do hope not. Pulling together is the aim of despotism and tyranny. Free men pull in all kinds of directions."

— Terry Pratchett, The Truth

7 Use clearing meetings to advance self-organization

This chapter discusses how to use the idea of a clearing meeting to advance the team slowly toward the ability and skills needed to solve their own problems without you. I've found this technique useful in my own teams.

In the previous chapters, you learned about the learning phase. In this chapter, you learn how to slowly move your team into self-organization while measuring your progress. To reiterate, self-organization is achieved when everyone on the team learns how to solve their own problems and they don't need you to solve their problems for them. One crucial tool that I've found invaluable in driving the team toward a state of self-organization is *clearing meetings*.

I first learned about clearing meetings when one of my managers introduced the idea to our management team. He then implemented this as a standard weekly meeting for our team, and I've experienced this for more than two years with my own team as well as with other teams.

Clearing meetings can have several goals:

- To introduce important issues everyone should know about

- To pull the "andon cord," a stop-the-line trigger that makes everyone pay attention to an important issue and do something about it
- To give everyone the chance to air issues that bother them
- To gauge the current level of the team's self-organization
- To create more trust within the team
- To flex the team's self-organization muscles and remind them to solve problems on their own

It's called a clearing meeting because you uncover all the stuff the team knows is not working, any bad feelings they're keeping buried about the job, and actual information that should be shared. And then you actually do something about it.

To understand how it works, let me describe a typical session:

7.1 The Meeting

9 a.m Meeting Room

Present: Jim (team leader of team 1), Jenna (team leader of team 2), David (marketing team leader), and me.

Me: "Morning everyone. As usual, we're having this clearing meeting just like any other Friday. Remember that nothing is out of scope for discussion here and that I expect you to speak up if you disagree with something you hear. We're starting just like any other meeting, by going around the room with our usual set of questions. Jim, is there anything that you would have liked to have gone better this week? Something you're not happy about that happened?"

Jim: (Thinking...) "Hmm. As you know, our team was all set for a new release this week. Well, we failed to do a release even though that's something we committed to do. I know we tried our best, but something just wasn't clicking. I hated how we just went and deployed things manually instead of fixing the build script. I think that is what eventually stopped us from releasing."

Me: "OK. What are you going to do about it?"

Jim: (A little taken aback. Thinking...) "Well... hmm... I... I think we need to fix the build before doing anything else."

Me: "So you will...?"

Jim: "I will fix the build."

Me: "By...?"

Jim: "I will fix the build by this evening."

Me: "Is that really something you can commit to? Do you know exactly what's wrong with it that you're so sure it will take that long?"

Jim: "Well, I'm just guessing."

Me: "In that case, please commit to something fully under your control. For example, that you will spend X hours on it in the next couple of days until it is solved. Or something like that."

Jim: "Yeah, makes sense. I will work on fixing the build at least five hours each day of the week until it works the way it should."

Me: "Are you happy with that solution, Jim?"

Jim: "Mmhmm. Yep!"

Jenna: "Jim, if you fix the build, you're doing that thing again. That thing where you take on everything yourself because you hate wasting time explaining things to other people. That hurts my team, because whenever they need something from your team, they usually get referred to *you*, since your team doesn't know how to do anything but the simplest tasks."

Jim: "Yeah, I get it. You also said that in the last meeting. But, seriously, we don't have time for teaching everyone on my team about the build process."

Jenna: (Sighs.) "This sucks. You'll say the same thing in the next meeting and the one after that. Aren't we supposed to be agile?"

Me: "Sounds like survival mode to me."

Jim: (Sighs.) "I didn't realize it until I heard the words coming out of my mouth."

Me: "So what are you going to do about *that*?"

Jim: "I'll need to make more time so the team can learn about the builds."

Me: (Smiling.) "So you will...by...?"

Jim: "I will remove or change enough commitments by the end of next week, so that there is enough time for me to teach at least one person about the build. And then the week after, on Monday, I will pair on the build with Christie, I think. She always seemed interested in how the build works anyway."

Me: "OK. Are you happy with that solution?"

Jim: (Thinking...) "Yes, I think that's a step in the right direction."

Me: "OK, Thanks Jim. Jenna, anything that wasn't working for you this week?"

Jenna: "Well, there was this one thing, but I'm already doing something about it."

Me: "Great! If you wanna share, feel free."

Jenna: "Well, not really. It was something between me and another person and we weren't getting along, but I talked with them this morning, and we're working on patching things out."

Me: "Happy to hear. David, anything you'd like to share that maybe hasn't worked well for you this week?"

David: "No. Nothing special."

Me: "Really? Everything was just perfect? This week couldn't have gone better at work?"

David: (Wrapped in thought...) "Well, you know, I think we're building the wrong product."

Jim: "What do you mean?"

David: "It's a long story. Let's take this offline. It's just going to make this meeting too long."

Me: "No, please continue. If it bothers you, the team needs to hear this, and we might need to do something about it."

Jim: "Is this about that customer mirror test?" (Where you see a customer using your product behind a mirror.)

David: "Yeah. From what I saw on Tuesday, people are trying to use our product more like we initially thought they might rather than how we've been designing it over the last couple of months. I have many doubts about it."

Jenna: "So you're saying we should drop it all and go back to the two-month-old idea? Seriously? All that time wasted?"

David: "I'm not saying..."

Jim: "David, you've only been here six months. You might be seeing things through rose-colored glasses."

David: "Well, actually, that might not be a bad thing. But, before changing everything, let me show you the videos."

(David runs and gets his laptop, and shows about five minutes' worth of his video highlights.)

David: "Now, what do you think?"

Jim: "Yeah, that was NOT good."

David: "Exactly."

Me: "OK, David, so what are you going to do about it?"

David: "Well, I want to be more sure. I want to run some more customer tests."

Me: "So you will...?"

David: "That's it, I can't do anything about that. I don't own the budget. That's you."

Me: "I have to say I'm not convinced. We might be seeing too little. We might need more tests."

David: "If you approve, I'll make calls to the company that sets these up and arrange for three more sessions by the end of today."

Me: "OK, do that."

(I write myself a note about the budget.)

Me: "OK, David, so are you happy with this start of a solution?"

David: "Yep!"

Me: "OK then. Great. Now let's start with the second question. (I turn to Jim again.) Jim, tell us about something good that happened for you this week or something good that was done by someone you work with."

Jim: "Well, *Blaine* is back from being sick. And he's jazzed up. Today he was teaching everyone about regular expressions. I feel like we are getting our energy back with this guy around."

Me: "Great! Jenna? One good thing?"

Jenna: "I noticed that James from my team and Joyce from David's team were working together on some numbers for the product box a couple days ago. That's the first time I saw anyone from marketing talking to anyone but me on my team. It was great!"

Me: "Cool. David?"

David: "Yeah. That was nice huh? After we talked following last week's clearing meeting, I talked to Joyce and challenged her to talk to a real dev. He said it was weird, but in a good way. In any case, my good thing is about Jim. When he spoke to that annoyed customer from Coca-Cola the other day, that really saved my neck. Thanks for taking a personal look."

Jim: "Happy to help."

Me: "OK. What's not working for me? Well, nothing. Whatever wasn't working, you're already doing something about that. So for me, everything is working great. Jim, this week you and your team tried to do a feature we thought was next to impossible. You almost made it to release, and I think next week when it *is* released, it will be amazing. Thanks. Jenna, thank you for doing such an amazing job bringing two new people into your team at such difficult times. You're spending time with them instead of in meetings, and that's commendable. Thank you. David, you guys brought in one of the clients we lost a year ago. Great job! OK, everybody. Does everybody know what they are going to do once they leave this room?"

(Everyone nods.)

Jim: "Um... Wait. So what will I do again?"

Jenna: "You will make time to teach your team about builds and then pair up. Next week."

Jim: "Ah, cool, Jenna. Good memory. Nice!"

Everyone leaves.

7.2 What just happened?

You've just read a not-so-remote account of something that happened on a real team I was on. The team had a passionate discussion about things that needed to change, and people took responsibility for their own problems. The meeting ended with everyone knowing what they are going to do and hopefully feeling that things were already on the way to improvement.

To understand and analyze this meeting, we have to take a step back and talk about integrity and how that fits with what happened.

7.3 What is integrity again?

I discussed the idea of integrity in the chapter about commitment language.

In this meeting, I was using commitment language and making sure people are in full integrity with what they are promising.

When people were promising something they could'nt fully control, I brought them back to reality by asking them to commit to a more realistic set of actions that will bring them to their goal.

For exampe, when they commited to fix a bug by a specific time I asked them to commit to working on it X hours each day instead.

Let's get a better handle on what happened by looking at the overall structure I used for the meeting.

The structure of the meeting

The structure that worked for me follows a rather simplistic process and can take anywhere from 30 minutes to a few hours, depending on how burning and passionate the issues discussed are:

- "What has *not* been working for you this past week?"
- Possibly having "detours" during the answers
- "What are you going to do about it?"
- "What has been working for you the past week?"
- Your closing words

Let's take a closer look.

The meeting

I started the integrity meeting by asking these three simple questions, going around the room with each one before moving to the next one.

"What has *not* been working for you this past week?"

This question is very open ended. The idea is to see if there is anything that has been missed either at the personal or team level. People can get frustrated with so many things in the software world, and if you let them talk about things that frustrated them, even if they feel small, you might be surprised at how much they're willing to share.

Things that you might look for are:

- "The build keeps failing."
- "Documentation sucks."
- "Team X is giving us a hard time."
- "We are doing the wrong thing."

These or other things related to the current work environment, people, or process are valid. Looking at this question from the self-organization point of view, this question is really asking, **"Is there anything that hurts the team and needs correcting?"**

However, it is a question that the people being asked should learn to ask themselves. *You* are asking this question because it's part of the almost invisible process of training people to think about the current status quo and continuously contemplate what next changes should be done. Avoiding blind acceptance of the status quo is one of the things you want your team to learn.

People might at first say, "Nothing went badly this week." Try to persist a little bit. Give examples of what it might sound like. Try not to accept "nothing" for an answer, especially from the first couple of people being asked. Other people in the meeting will follow the lead of the first few and, if the first ones are silent, will shy from saying anything, most of the time.

Also note that this kind of question can raise some demons that might have been previously been kept in backroom meetings. If an argument starts, try to keep it going. Embrace conflict. People who have been heard are more willing to make a commitment even if they don't like the decision made by the group or the leader.

"What are you going to do about it?"

If a person has indicated that something was not going well this week, ask them, "What are you going to do about it?" You may ask in a more polite manner, but remember what we talked about in the chapter about commitment language: don't use words with a way out. Here are some examples that give a way out by asking the question in a different way:

- "What *could* you do about it?" (A mere contemplation vs. request for a specific action.)
- "How *would* you fix it?" (Again, a contemplation vs. an actual request for action.)

Once you have challenged the person about action, make sure you get all the way to a commitment. That person needs to know what they are going to do after the meeting is over or have a timeline or end date they are expected to act by.

From the point of view of self-organization, this is an important learning tool for the person being asked. *Always* couple, "What are you going to do about it?" with a statement that something is not going well. Too many times we simply complain about the world and don't do anything about it. Here's a situation that's much closer to us—our own work—and we (the person being asked) have much more personal say over how things really work around us. We can influence our immediate environment and we should.

For a self-organizing team, having the personal realization for each team member, that they are not simply *stuck* in a situation but can always choose to do something about it, is one of those turnaround moments. A team can begin turning proactive instead of reactive. A team can begin anticipating and preventing problems, and people on the team can stop thinking they have to be miserable to do their jobs.

You can teach your team that, as professionals, it's OK for them to feel annoyed at the way things are. They *should* be feeling happier when things are being done more professionally. Then they *should* take those gut feelings they have and apply them toward making a better work environment, product, and process.

So the core lesson here, again is:

> Do not blindly accept that which bothers you.
> There is always *something* you can do.

This question, normally in connection with a problem state-ment, is a core lesson: the skill you are teaching is for them to ask themselves this question when something bothers them.

This is the core of self-organization: when the team finds something that needs to change, they look *within* to begin solving the problem, instead of forwarding the problem to a manager.

"What has been working for you the past week?"

Once you've gone around the room and all the bad energy has been emptied, and you've made sure anyone who had a problem is doing something about it, start asking this question.

There are several reasons for this question for each person answering:

- Clear the air and have a positive feeling.
- Acknowledge people for their actions and efforts.
- Share good news and information with the team.

Try to make the answer about other people in the team or company, but don't force it. Here are some examples of answers I hear:

- "I sat with X from the QA department and, for the first time, it was really helpful."
- "I pair-programmed with X and we found something I was stuck on for a while. It felt good."

- "We finally released that thing we were stuck on."
- "We got new machines! Finally!"

There should *always* be something good to say. Don't let people not say anything. If they cannot think of something, return to them at the end of the round. This is a lesson in noticing others and being social enough to share a compliment.

Your closing words

Now that everyone has said what didn't work and what did work for them this week, it's your turn. You answer the first question: "What didn't work for me this week?" Now, it's possible that there was something that really didn't work for you this week and you still haven't begun doing anything about it. This is a good time to bring it up with your team and say what you're going to do about it.

For example:

> "This week I noticed that I spent way too much time on meetings instead of being there with you when you needed me. Like when the build crashed and you waited for me a whole day. So what am I going to do about it? I will block off at least 50 percent of my time in the coming month in the company calendar, so that I don't get this distracted again. I'll do this by the end of the day today."

Also, as closing words, remind the team that, as an exercise, you want them to try to reach the next meeting not only with things that didn't work for them but also with actions they've already taken. It can go something like this:

"Next week, the day before the meeting, imagine the meeting has started and I'm asking you what didn't work well this week. Then imagine your answer and my follow-up question, "What are you going to do about it?" Then, answer that question in your head, commit to an action, and then just do it. Ideally, you should come to the next meeting saying, "There was X that bothered me, but I'm already doing something about it.""

The overall point of this meeting

As discussed at the beginning of this chapter, this meeting can be used for many things. I find that it is very effective at teaching a team of peers to think proactively about solving things that bother them and at the same time gauging just how self-reliant they are.

Each meeting, see how many people say, "I had a problem with X but I'm already doing something about it." The day everyone says it, you can say your team is self-organizing. They are proactively solving their own problems without waiting for anyone else's permission to do anything about it.

7.4 Keeping the meeting on track

What happens if you notice personal attacks, stubbornness, helplessness or other negative behaviors in the meeting? If you haven't had many meetings yet, this could just be the underlying team dysfunctions appearing before your eyes.

If this is the first time this has happened, or the first meeting, sit back and perhaps write notes about behaviors you found problematic.

I would not necessarily do anything to stop things. If a new member in the team suggests changes and gets attacked in the meeting, let them handle the fire on their own. Don't stop the meeting and take things offline. Let the team member learn how to handle themselves in a team argument. Later, after the meeting, you can sit with them in a one on one meeting, and coach them on handling future meetings better.

Conflict is not bad in such meetings. In fact, if you have no conflict, you might not be talking about the truly important subjects.

A beta reader asked if seeing those behaviors means the team is not mature enough to have that meeting. I think that the purpose of the meeting is to take an immature team and make it more mature. So making the team stay away from the meeting until the right time is just prolonging the wait for a mature team.

Next up

Next, we will go into the "notes" part of this book. I hope that the first half of the book's overview of elastic leadership principles, the three team phases, the leadership styles and techniques will be helpful for you down the road. Enjoy the notes!

8 Influence Patterns

A big part of the frustration I have felt, and that you might be feeling, is about helplessness. You believe in doing the right things, but you just can't seem to get the people around you to change their behavior.

> What about using my authority?

Using your authority is usually the path you should take *last*, unless you're in survival mode. Then, using authority is the *second* best choice after having people intrinsically motivated to be doing something differently.

Also, when it comes time for the learning and self-organization phase, telling people *what* to do is a very ineffective way to teach. Helping them find their own path that makes everyone win is a much more effective way to teach new skills.

I'm going to borrow some important vocabulary from a great book called *Influencer - The power to change anything*, by Kerry Patterson, Joseph Grenny, David Maxfield, Ron McMillan, and Al Switzler. The book details a very powerful technique to help you discover what you can do to change behavior in others.

When I teach this technique in my workshops, I remind students that the most important thing before they start this exercise is to find a demonstrable physical behavior that they would like to change. Examples might include:

- Team member X is always late to the stand-up meeting.
- X never asks for help when he is stuck on a task.
- X does not participate in any offer to pair-program.
- X does not write unit tests.

Now, here are some bad examples:

- X thinks he knows things better than everyone else. (You cannot know what a person thinks or feels, and this is not a physical behavior.)
- X always argues. (Be more specific. When we meet on Z, X argues more than X minutes.)
- X does not like to work on this project. (This is not a behavior you can target for change.)

So, what do you if you really want to be able to change a *core behavior* (such as those detailed above)?

The book details six influence forces:

Category	Forces
Personal	Personal ability
	Personal motivation
Social	Social ability
	Social motivation
Environmental	Environmental ability
	Environmental motivation

I know that I and some others think of only the first two forces (personal ability and personal motivation) when we try to understand why a person is not doing anything. Because our profession requires us to think as logically as possible, many times we think that if we only explain a subject or a reason, then that someone will immediately "convert" to our point of view. We are then stumped when that does not happen:

> "I sent him on a two-day unit-testing course and explained all the benefits of unit testing. He is obviously lazy or doesn't care about the project."

This is what happens when we run out of options to consider: we start looking at dark crevices in our mind and start putting words in people's mouths without even asking them. Many times, we play this "I know what he'll say" game *because* we are afraid to talk face to face with that person about what truly bothers us.

Maybe not entirely consciously, but it's hard to deny that this happens to many of us. Remember, it is *your job* to do all the hard stuff, and that includes gently confronting people and talking with them about serious issues. This has to be done in a personal setting (a one-on-one meeting), but it does need to be done.

Let's walk through each of the influence forces.

Force	Description
Personal ability	Does the person have all the skills or knowledge to perform what is required?
Personal motivation	Does the person take satisfaction from the right behavior or dislike the wrong behavior?

Force	Description
Social ability	Do they have the self-control to engage in the behavior when it's hardest to do so?
Social motivation	Do you or others provide the help, information, and resources required to that person, particularly at critical times?
	Are the people around them actively encouraging the right behavior ..
	..or discouraging the wrong behavior?
	Are you or others modeling the right behavior in an effective way?
Environmental ability	Are there aspects in the environment (building, budget, and so on)..
	..that make the behavior convenient, easy, and safe?
	Are there enough cues and reminders to the stay on course?
Environmental motivation	Are there clear and meaningful rewards (such as with pay, bonuses, or incentives)..

Force	Description
	..when you or others behave the right or wrong way? Do short-term rewards match the desired long-term results.. ..and behaviors you want or want to avoid?

Now that you have the basic list of rules, let's see how you can use them in real life.

An imaginary example, using our new checklist

Here is an example of an imaginary checklist I have made about someone not performing TDD (keep in mind that this differs for each person in each organization).

Force	Description
Personal ability	Yes. They went through a three day TDD course with Roy Osherove.
Personal motivation	I spoke with them and they like doing TDD.
Social ability	No problem.
Social motivation	As much as possible.
Environmental ability	* - We Don't have a budget for a build machine
Environmental motivation	* - When we try to spend time unit testing, our managers tell us we are wasting time...

Force	Description
	..If we ship early with lower quality, we get a bonus.

I put asterisks next to the items in the right column that require work. Here I've identified two issues that need to be resolved. Solving only the build machine budget problem will not change the behavior. We have to do two things. First, we have to get a build machine. Second, we need to convince our managers to stop giving bonuses to people who ship quickly with very poor quality.

> For the behavior to change, you must change all the factors in play. If you change just one of them, the behavior won't change.

A note about privacy: Never discuss private matters with that person or other people publicly. Talk in a one-on-one setting, because it can be very hurtful for people to be confronted or asked a personal question in public.

I hope this short chapter helps you figure out what is wrong. Next up, we have notes written by other leaders, just like you, and by some consultants I trust.

The only thing that this entire remaining section proves is that everyone is making it up as they go.

V Notes to a software team leader

"Imitation is not just the sincerest form of flattery - it's the sincerest form of learning." — George Bernard Shaw

There are so many people I have come to know and respect in our industry. I have collected some thoughts of some of them in this part of the book. I asked them "what is one thing you would teach a new team leader that they must know to succeed?"

Along the way, several other leaders and consultants had some great ideas for notes to include, and the end result is a combined piece of knowledge that I hope you will find helpful, interesting and thought provoking.

Roy.

9 Feeding Back by Kevlin Henney

About Kevlin: Kevlin is an independent consultant and trainer with an interest in programming,
patterns, practice and process. He has been a
columnist for a number of magazines and web
sites, not all of which have folded, and is the
co-author of *A Pattern Language for Distributed
Computing* and *On Patterns and Pattern Languages*, two volumes in the *Pattern-Oriented Software Architecture* series. He is also the editor
of *97 Things Every Programmer Should Know*.
Kevlin speaks at conferences, lives online and in
transit, and writes short fiction in what perhaps
qualifies as his spare time.

A slim figure takes to the stage, dressed in orange and black,
wreathed in a bandana, his guitar flipped over and strung for
left-handed play. It's the close of over three days of hedonistic
and culturally shifting psychedelia and sound. Humans have
recently and for the first time set foot in another world.

It's 1969. It's Woodstock. It's Jimi Hendrix. During his set he
splices metallic whale song into his fluid solos, coaxing sounds
from his Stratocaster that guitars simply have no business
making.

This is feedback. Not the negative feedback that dampens
sound and enthusiasm. Positive feedback. But not gushing and

uncontrolled, neither excessive nor insincere. There is an art to feedback.

Feedback, especially positive feedback, is normally a sound engineer's nightmare. A skilled guitarist can make it part of the performance, part of the music. For software engineers, offering and taking feedback, positive or negative, can be just as much a minefield. When there is a problem, it is too easy to resort to silence or complaint. When there isn't a problem, it is too easy to resort to silence.

When you ride a bicycle, feedback is essential. Sight, hearing and proprioception allow you to navigate and balance, to respond to the bike and the road. You respond when the bike is balanced and on a steady course: you respond by continuing to do what you are doing, preserving your course and your balance. You respond when the bike loses balance, destabilized perhaps by a hole or a bump. You change behaviour, you react to recover and put the bike back on course. And you respond when the situation on the road changes. You avoid pedestrians, cars and other bikes, stop at junctions and red lights, cycle more carefully in the rain.

Part of team leadership involves leading by example, but part involves guidance. For simple systems, guidance is programmatic, a matter of command and control. This doesn't work well for complex systems, and individuals and teams are very complex systems indeed. Feedback is a guidance technique, but there is an art to it that goes beyond the simple presentation of the facts as you see them. To be effective, feedback also needs to be trusted, concrete, and constructive.

No matter how upstanding they might be, we do not generally consider people to be objective sources of information in the way that inanimate objects and software tools are. When a piece of code fails a test or doesn't compile, we do not attribute this to a subjective judgement of the test or the emotional state of the compiler (unless we're having a really bad day). When we get feedback from people, we are more likely to hear what they are saying through a veil of emotions, cognitive biases, and relationships.

If the only feedback you offer is negative and corrective, it is likely to dampen anyone's spirits, independently of whether or not it is factually correct. Negative feedback is likely to breed mistrust and resentment. It is disempowering and demotivating. The absence of any positive feedback, by implication, suggests that there is nothing the person is doing right.

Relentless feedback of any one form does not offer the guidance or build the trust that will help you, the individual or the team. This applies just as much to unconditional positive feedback as it does to negative feedback. Positive feedback is psychologically necessary; otherwise, people feel like they're operating in a vacuumâ€"-the few humans who have ever been privileged to work in a literal rather than figurative vacuum know that support is a necessity, not an optionâ€"-but there is a balance to be struck: excessive and unwarranted positive feedback simply becomes saccharine and insincere.

Feedback should also be contextual and concrete. Simply saying someone's work is good is a pat on the back, but it's vague and there is little guidance, little they can take away from it beyond feeling congratulated. What is it that is good? Whether we are talking about someone overcoming a personal or technical challenge, meeting a goal or fielding ideas, be specific. Unless you are specific, it is difficult for them to know what is good about what they did so that they can learn from it, repeat it, and build on it.

It is this question of learning and allowing someone else to do the learning that highlights the weakness of negative feedback. Even without the question of self-esteem, simply pointing out that something is not good is not helpful, and in this case adding detail doesn't help. Just saying something is not good does not tell someone what is good. There is little they can learn from it. It's like a no-entry sign on a one-way street: you are told which way you should not go, but you are not told which way you should go.

Negative feedback is often given in response to seeing a problem, but it is not intrinsically problem solving and constructive. To be constructive, you need to offer a concrete suggestion for improvement or you need to make the giving of feedback part of a problem-solving conversation. If you want someone to learn, create the opportunity and environment for them to discuss and contribute; otherwise, the feedback becomes more about the person giving the feedback than the person receiving it. Feedback should have purpose and it should enable purpose.

Feedback, as a term, is often taken to be unidirectional but, as its engineering origins suggest, it is definitely about a relationship. It involves guidance and balance. Steady as she goes.

10 Channel conflict into learning by Dan North

About Dan North: Dan is an independent technology consultant who writes software and coaches teams and organisations in Agile and Lean methods. He believes in putting people first and writing simple, pragmatic software.

Difference of opinion in high-performing teams isn't necessarily a bad thing. In fact, conflict is a necessary ingredient of learning teams. In his book *The Fifth Discipline*, Peter Senge describes the twin discourse activities of dialogue, where a team explores an idea from a number of perspectives, and discussion, where they attempt to reach consensus. If everyone agrees all of the time, there isn't any stimulus for growth.

On the other hand, conflict between strong personalities can be difficult to manage and can cause factions or cliques within a team and eventually tear it apart. As a software team leader, it will fall to you to make the big decisions: Which technologies should we adopt? Which of these competing frameworks should we choose? When the team senses change on the horizon, you will find strong advocates for different alternatives, which can paralyse the team.

When I find a team blocked on a decision, I will often suggest deferring the commitment by trying all the options simultaneously and letting the data inform the decision. On one occasion, a team leader asked me whether his experienced Java team should adopt Clojure or Scala as their "next generation" JVM language. The team had agreed they wanted to stay on the JVM but move beyond Java and had reached a stalemate over which direction to take. He was feeling pressured because, in his words, he had to make a decision imminently, both from a team health perspective and because the stalling was beginning to impact their delivery. My answer surprised him:

- "Should we go with Clojure or Scala?"
- "Yes"
- "Eh?"

There were six developers in his team, so I suggested they go with Clojure and Scala. And Java! At least for the next couple of weeks or so. One pair would learn Scala, one Clojure, and the third pair would stick with Java.

They would all work on the same features, which means they would be coding in a real domain rather than playing with code katas or tutorials, and within a couple of weeks they would have some real data to make a decision with.

How easy was it to learn the language? How well was it suited to the problem at hand? How did each of the approaches compare with one another? How nicely did they integrate with the existing codebase? How important were each of these things in this context? They would also have the Java solution as a control for comparison.

This approach uses an idea from the manufacturing industry called Concurrent Set-Based Engineering: several suppliers build the same thing, say an airplane wing, in different ways, and after a while you choose one of them to take forward. You still pay the others-â€"this exercise is at your expense rather than theirs-â€"but it means that regardless of which you choose you haven't lost any time. You are trading off efficiency for effectiveness: it's more expensive to get there, but you get there faster and you know you made a better decision. Many safety-critical industries mandate this approach for certain components.

The team leader added a nice twist to this. Halfway through he got the pairs to switch round, so by the end of the experiment each pair had tried two of the languages. After a couple of weeks the team reached a strong consensus around one of the choices. They had found it a better fit for their specific context, both in terms of the language itself and its libraries and toolchain. The team was unblocked and, what's more, they had reached the decision as a team and learned about the alternatives along the way.

11 It's Probably Not a Technical Problem - Bill Walters

About Bill: Bill has been working in software and testing for a long time. He's attended the Jerry Weinberg PSL workshop and read a number of his books and articles and can, therefore, be labeled as a biased disciple.

I learned this from Jerry Weinberg, somewhere. The most difficult problems are not technical problems. As a rule of thumb, when you step back and look at the problem you are facing, chances are the real issue is not a technical one; it's probably a nonrational, subconscious soul-fart, that is bubbling around inside somewhere, masking as a technical problem.

It's not really that this person doesn't understand how the wobbulator is supposed to work, it's that the person doesn't understand, and there's a stigma or expectation that they should, and, therefore, the fear of being kicked out of the tribe is lurking somewhere beneath the surface.

12 Review the Code by Robert C. Martin (Uncle Bob)

About Robert: Robert Martin (Uncle Bob) has been a programmer since 1970. He is the Master Craftsman at 8th Light inc, and the author of many books including: The Clean Coder, Clean Code, Agile Software Development: Principles, Patterns, and Practices, and UML for Java Programmers. He is a prolific writer and has published hundreds of articles, papers, and blogs. He served as the Editor-in-chief of the C++ Report, and as the first chairman of the Agile Alliance.

One of the biggest mistakes that new software team leaders make is to consider the code written by the programmers as the private property of the author, as opposed to an asset owned by the team. This causes the team leaders to judge code based on its behavior rather than its structure. Team leaders with this dysfunction will accept any code so long as it does what it is supposed to do, regardless of how it is written. Indeed, such team leaders often don't bother to read the other programmers' code at all. They satisfy themselves with the fact that the system works and divorce themselves from system structure.

This is how you lose control over the quality of your system. And, once you lose that control, the software will gradually degrade into an unmaintainable morass. Estimates will grow, defect rates will climb, morale will decline, and eventually everyone will be demanding that the system be redesigned.

A good team leader takes responsibility for the code structure as well as its behavior. A good team leader acts as a quality inspector, looking at *every* line of code written by any of the programmers under their lead. A good team leader rejects a fair bit of that code and asks the programmers to improve the quality of that code.

A good team leader maintains a vision of code quality. They will communicate that vision to the rest of the team by ensuring that the code they personally write conforms to the highest quality standards and by reviewing all of the other code in the system and rejecting the code that does not meet those exacting standards.

As teams grow, good team leaders will recruit lieutenants to help them with this review and enforcement task. The lieutenants review *all* the code, and the team leader falls back on reviewing *all* the code written by the lieutenants and spot checking the code written by everyone else.

Code is a team asset, not personal property. No programmer should ever be allowed to keep their code private. Any other programmer on the team should have the right to improve that code at any time. And the team leader must take responsibility for the overall quality of that code. The team leader must communicate and enforce a consistent vision of high quality and professional behavior.

13 Document Your Air, Food, and Water by Travis Illig

About Travis: Travis Illig is a .NET developer who enjoys the art of solving problems with technology. He currently is a Senior Software Developer with Fiserv, working on next-generation online banking products. He holds a BS in Computer Science from Portland State University and is a Microsoft Certified Solutions Developer (MCSD) for .NET. Travis can be contacted through his blog at http://www.paraesthesia.com.

Think about all of the things you need to know when you're new to a team. There are a lot of things, right?

- Where is the source code repository?
- Which tools need to be installed on your developer environment?
- What are the steps to build the product?
- Is there a pattern for how the code is laid out in the repository?
- How are tasks tracked?

- What is the task branch pattern in the repository?
- Where is the continuous integration server?
- Are there any specific development methodologies that should be followed?

...And so on. This is, from a peer mentoring perspective[1], the "Air, Food, and Water" for the group. It's the stuff you need to know in order to basically get around.

Many times, the answers to these questions aren't actually documented anywhere. It's "tribal knowledge." People just sort of "know" what needs to be done, and if you don't know, you ask the group. That sort of approach might work well in a small group that doesn't change a lot... but what about in a larger group? Does everyone actually know? Or is there a slightly different understanding of how things work from person to person? And what about new team members?

It's a good idea to **document your air, food, and water** in a central location that's accessible to everyone. Keep sort of a "team FAQ" that has the answers to all of these questions and make sure everyone knows where it is. It doesn't have to be reams of heavy documentation, but it should contain enough to clearly answer the questions.

Why document?

- **Enable team members to help themselves.** It's generally understood[2] that "quick questions" causing team members to task switch are actually not as "free" as one might think[3]. If there's a place that folks can go to

---

[1] http://www.peermentoring.com/
[2] http://www.codinghorror.com/blog/archives/000691.html
[3] http://www.fastcompany.com/articles/2008/07/interview-gloria-mark.html

answer simple questions, it reduces context switches, particularly when there are newer members on the team.

- **Give new team members confidence in the team.** Last time you joined a team, how was the experience? Did it seem a little jarring or was it really smooth? When you're new to a team it's like meeting a person for the first time... and you only get one chance for a first impression. Wouldn't it be nice to join a team and have the reassurance that there's a plan and a simple document that lays out everything you need to know to get going? If you saw that, wouldn't you gain a little confidence in the team?

- **Add visibility into your team.** If there are other people or teams in your company that are interested in seeing how you're doing things (maybe to learn something from your team?), having a document makes it easy for them to see how things are done and understand what they're looking at.

How do you get started? How do you maintain it?

1. **Find a location.** Find a central place on your company's network that you can store the document such that everyone has access to it. Maybe it's a wiki. Maybe it's a SharePoint site. Maybe it's a simple file share. As long as everyone has access to it, it's perfect.

2. **Document as you get asked questions.** As people have questions about how the team works—where the source code is, and so on, refer them to the document. If the answer isn't there, consider adding the answer to the document and providing the document to the

person asking the question. Eventually you'll have a document with the answers to the most frequently asked questions about the team.

3. **Pass it by exiting team members.** Team members come in, and team members move on. Before a team member moves on from the team, part of the knowledge transfer should be having them review the document and fill in applicable answers. There may be some things that team member was responsible for that no one else really knows about.

4. **Give it to new team members.** When a new member comes on board, give them the document as a way to get them set up. It will quickly become apparent if the information on the document is incomplete. When incomplete/incorrect information is encountered, have the new team member work with the team to find out the correct information and update the document.

5. **Update as changes occur.** As changes are made in the way the team works, update the document to reflect them. There shouldn't be so much information there that it's overwhelming to maintain, but the doc does need to be a living entity, just as your team is.

Make sure to **keep your document fairly lightweight and easy to maintain.** If it's too thick or complex, if information is repeated in multiple places throughout, people will skip updating it and eventually it will become stale. You don't want thatâ€"you want it to be easy so when it's time to update, it's *simple, simple, simple.*

It doesn't take much and it pays off in spades. Why not start today?

14 Appraisals and Agile Don't Play Nicely by Gary Reynolds

The following is a guest post by Gary Reynolds[a]. Gary is a Development Manager for a global software company, with particular expertise in transitioning teams from traditional software development practices to more agile ways of working.

[a]http://agilisation.blogspot.com/

Appraisals, performance reviews, 360 feedback, evaluations—call them what you will—have been present in organizations in one form or another for over 100 years. Over this time, the process has taken a number of different forms, depending on the current trends and the size of the organization.

I personally have experience of written evaluations where the employee has no input, various rating systems where both employees and managers get to rate the individual, and written appraisals where the employee makes comments on their own performance that are then used as the basis for further discussion. Some systems have been directly linked to pay and promotion opportunities whereas some have been explicitly decoupled.

One thing that they all have in common is that they focus on the individual, their performance, and what they've accomplished since the last review period. They encourage the individual to take credit for themselves and to compete against the other people on their team for recognition and a limited pot of money when it comes to bonuses and salary increases.

I would suggest that this is in direct conflict with the adoption and use of agile frameworks within the organization.

Think about that:

- Agile emphasizes teamwork and co-operation in order to successfully deliver a product, with individuals being prepared to take on any task that needs doing in order to complete the iteration and get to "done." Individual accountability, as valued by the traditional appraisal system, implies that individuals should be interested in taking the juiciest or most challenging tasks for themselves in order to prove their worth and progress within the organization.
- Agile emphasizes the forming of self-organizing teams who direct and manage their own work, whereas appraisals involve the setting of objectives that traditionally come from the manager.
- Agile processes emphasize continual process improvement and, while this can be done alongside traditional appraisals, appraisals are geared more toward making individual or process changes at review time.

Is there a case for abolishing appraisals altogether in an agile environment? Well, perhaps. The challenge is that individuals within an organization expect and deserve feedback on their performance.

Perhaps a step in the right direction would be for team leaders to make the appraisal process itself more agile and encourage an environment where the annual review is replaced or supplemented with a system of continuous feedback and learning where individuals—in line with agile—are empowered to self-organize their own career development. Here are some ideas to get you started:

- Build learning and career development into individual user stories, perhaps in the form of a specific task that involves team members expanding their business domain knowledge. Alternatively, include time for learning tasks into your velocity calculations so you can increase the "value" of each team member to the organization by expanding their skillset in a way that's relevant to their immediate task. Let the individuals drive and organize this learning process as they would a normal development task.
- Encourage pairing (pair-programming for example) on tasks that help individuals to learn from those more experienced than them.
- Include team member feedback sessions as part of your iteration retrospective process, where you can directly discuss what people have learnt.
- Encourage individuals, on an iteration-by-iteration basis, to maintain a body of evidence that can be directly referenced at formal appraisal time. This will reduce the time taken to plan and perform the appraisal and encourages the recording of tasks at the time they happen—when they're most relevant.

140Appraisals and Agile Don't Play Nicely by Gary Reynolds

What else can you think of?

15 Leading Through Learning: The Responsibilities of a Team Leader by Cory Foy

AboutCory Foy[a]: Cory Foy is an agile coach and developer living in Bayonet Point, FL. He is currently helping product teams become much more lean in their approaches to building product through the focused use of both craftsmanship and agile practices and principles. Prior to his current role, Cory worked with teams around the globe bringing agile and development best practices to Microsoft customers as a Senior PFE. He has also been involved in several start-up organizations where delivering high value while keeping the code clean is vital. When not spending time with his wife and two girls, Cory enjoys working as the global community liaison for the Scrum Alliance, speaking at conferences and user groups, and playing guitar, drums, or whatever he can get his hands on. He can be found at http://www.cornetdesign.com or on Twitter at @cory_-

foy.

———————

[a]http://www.cornetdesign.com/

I was honored when Roy asked me to explore the topic of team leadership. And it's an interesting topic too since it can cover such a broad array of things.

And while we could cover the normal things (servant leadership, impediment removal, motivation), there is one thing I think intrinsically sets great leaders apart from mediocre ones.

To get there, we first should discuss the responsibility of a team member.

One of the things that has excited me the most about the Software Craftsmanship movement is a shift of responsibility. So many times we as developers have set out with the ingrained feeling that it is our organization's responsibility to help us grow and succeed. And this was true to some extent in the early days–great programmers stayed with great companies for a long time.

Growth was something you expected when you got hired in. You could look forward to being somewhere, putting in your best, and getting rewarded by retiring with them and being taken care of in return.

But, those days are gone. I don't know of any colleagues who have gotten hired by a company thinking that they would be there for 20 or 30 years. That seemingly coincides with the mantra of "Here today, gone tomorrow," which some organizations practice. That further means that, if we can't even be sure that our jobs are still going to be here, we can't certainly expect that organizations will help us grow as a matter of normalcy.

So, as a part of the Craftsmanship Movement, we've declared that one shouldn't expect to be getting knowledge from organizational initiatives or in the course of their role on a team. In fact, the core of the movement is that developers need to be taking responsibility for their own careers–learning, teaching, mentoring, speaking.

In this book, Roy explored the questions each team leader should ask themselves. In it, there was one key question that is perhaps the hardest question for many leads:

> Will my developers be better in a month or two than they were before? If not, how do I make that happen?

This question, above all others, is what has set the leads I lift up above others. It doesn't matter the industry–I saw it from software team leads as much as fire captains and other industries I've been involved in. How do I create learning opportunities that enable my team to grow?

This past weekend I went to BarCamp Tampa Bay[1] and got to see Steven Bristol[2] talk about starting up a company. In it, he mentioned how feedback loops affect growth. If you are single, and go up to someone and ask them out, one of three things will happen:

1. They'll say yes

---

[1] http://barcamptampabay.org/
[2] http://b.lesseverything.com/

2. They'll say no (or some variant, like slapping you upside the head)
3. They'll turn around and walk away without saying a word

Out of the three, which will you learn the most from? Which will cause you to grow the most? Which will leave you scratching your head?

Imagine now that you are a developer on a team. You email your team lead and ask about taking on a new initiative for the team. The next afternoon an announcement is made that one of the senior developers is going to be working on the initiative you just emailed about.

Baffling, huh? Imagine if, instead, the team lead emailed you back and told you that she had concerns because you hadn't been involved with FooBar and, so, for this initiative Senior Joe was going to take it, but have you work closely with Joe so that you can jump on the next one.

Or, imagine the team lead replied and said go for it and offered guidelines so you could know what kind of progress you were making. And let's say you took that and failed miserably. But, because of the team involvement, others were able to pick up the ball with you and help get it done.

That's what you want from a team lead. This, in many ways, is the essence of leadership. Providing opportunities for people to fall, but always within the context of the safety net of the team. Motivating not by fear or by money, but by passion that the team is always greater than any one developer can be. It is turning your day to day interactions into chances for growth and learning, and ultimately building a Learning

Organization[3].

It also means setting aside one's ego, one's pride to be able to go out and help others. Effective team leads aren't generally the rock star developers who put in 70 hour weeks because they are hard core. They are solid technical leaders–and solid *people* leaders.

For example, Scott Bellware had an article on the Chief Engineer role[4] in which he described the responsibilities and qualities of the chief engineer at Toyota. These included:

- Voice of the customer
- Architecture
- Exceptional engineering skills
- A hard-driving teacher, motivator, and disciplinarian, yet a patient listener
- An exceptional communicator
- Always ready to get his or her hands dirty

So, if you are thinking about leading a team or finding yourself thrust into that role, ask yourself–are you growing? Are you seeking opportunities for yourself? For the team? Are you listening–truly listening–to what your team is telling you? Or are you constantly impatient for them to finish so you can tell them the *right* answer? And, most importantly, what actions am I taking today to make my developers–my team–better one week, one month, one year from now?

In the answers to those questions lies the growth path for you as a leader. Keep growing, keep questioning and keep learning–so that your team does too.

---

[3]http://blog.scottbellware.com/2008/12/learning-organization.html
[4]http://blog.scottbellware.com/2008/12/chief-engineer.html

16 The Core Protocols Introduction by Yves Hanoulle

I'm Yves Hanoulle, your virtual Project coach[a] and you can reach me at blog at my training company[b] .net or follow me on Twitter[c]

[a]http://paircoaching.wordpress.com
[b]http://www.paircoaching.net/
[c]http://twitter.com/yveshanoulle/

Roy has asked me if I wanted to write about The Core Protocols[1]. I will start by explaining where these rules came from.

[1]http://www.mccarthyshow.com/online/

COURAGE

MAKING WISE CHOICES
WHILE FEELING FEAR

This story starts in 1995. Jim McCarthy wrote *Dynamics of Software Development*[2]. After this book was very well received in the software community, (I see it as one of the predecessors of agile), Jim and his wife Michele decided to leave Microsoft to hold workshops about building teams. They designed these workshops to be experimental. The course was not presented like a usual class: It was a simulated one week project. Part of the assignment of the project was for the students to come up with their own team rules.

After a year or so, Jim and Michele realized that some team patterns kept getting great results. So they decided to write these rules down and give them to the students attending

---

[2]http://www.librarything.com/work/84233/book/11105120

the next workshop. They have done that for the last 13 years. These patterns are now called The Core Protocols.

Some...heck, most of these rules feel strange at first. You might think, "This will never work:

- "In my company."
- "In my country."
- "With my wife."
- "With my kids."
- "In my team."

I'm asking you to suspend your disbelief, and instead, try a few of these out in a safe environment. You don't have to believe in the sea to get wet. You only have to get in.

In this note, I will cover "The Check-In Protocol" portion of The Core Protocols[3] which are available for download at http://alturl.com/b9fn[4].

One of the most effective and, consequently, one of the most controversial protocols is check-in.

In presentations, when I ask the audience, "Who has worked with a colleague that hides emotions?" almost everyone raises

---

[3]http://5whys.com/blog/the-core-protocols-introduction.html
[4]http://alturl.com/b9fn
[5]http://www.incentiveplus.co.uk/p/342-7834/Box-Full-of-Feelings.html

his or her hand. When I then ask if this has hindered productivity at work, almost all the hands stay up.

Yet a lot of people are still convinced that showing their
emotions at work is not "professional."

I find that the Check-In Protocol offers a powerful way to
show emotions in a mature way, both at work and in my
personal life. In a check-in, we state how we feel using 4 basic
emotions: mad, glad, sad, and afraid.

Let me give you an example:

> I'm checking in.
>
> "I'm GLAD that Roy has asked me to write these
> guest posts. I'm AFRAID to do so. I'm GLAD I
> can ask for help I'm AFRAID that the power of
> the protocols can only be understood by using
> them. I'm AFRAID, SAD that people will turn
> away without trying them. I'm GLAD to know
> that some will probably accept my invitation to
> try them. I'm *in*."

This is an example where I used the protocol to the letter.
When I use the protocols with people not familiar with The
Core, I might say:

> "Hello, welcome to this training, I'm Yves Hanoulle.
> I'm glad to see so many people. I'm afraid that
> this puts pressure on me to make it great. That is
> ok because I have done this a lot of times. I'm mad
> because my replacement phone does not work
> here in Canada. I'm sad because delivering this
> workshop means I will miss my kids for 5 days.

If you think that this won't work in your company, in your country, with your spouse, and so on, then you are not alone."

I had a similar reaction about using the protocol with my oldest son. I was having a chat with Michele (McCarthy). She asked me to try check-in with him. I told her that he was three and a half years old and that I thought that was too young. We finished the conversation with my promise I would try it. (I was still convinced it would not work). The next day Joppe came home with a card from school with these 4 emotions on it. I realized I was the reason it wasn't working. He already knew about the four emotions. I've been using it with him ever since.

Using check-in with Joppe has taught me a lot. One night he said, "I'm MAD, SAD that the babysitter will be here. And you guys are going out." At that time, my partner and I went out to dinner every Thursday. It was a Thursday, but that day we weren't going to go, and we hadn't told him. Typically, we only told him when we were going out on the day we did. He had already made the connection, though, that Thursday equals babysitter. I realized that evening that Joppe might only be 4 years old, but he was much more clever than I was giving him credit for.

Now for a work story:

One morning I had an argument with my partner before leaving for work. The discussion was stuck in my head as I drove. On top of that, a crazy truck driver almost drove me off the road. When I arrived to work, I realized I was not my rational self because of these two events. So when I came in, I told my colleagues, "Sorry if I overreact a little today; I had a discussion at home before leaving; I'm still puzzled about some of the things we said to each other. I'm also mad about a crazy truck driver that drove me off the road." Right then my colleague gave me 10 minutes of slack time. Also, because I had checked in, I immediately forgot about what had happened. I didn't remember until I got back in my car that evening. Without checking in, I would have been stuck on those thoughts and feelings all day, and my productivity would have been a fraction of what it was.

So I propose you try the Check-In Protocol at work and at home, and see how much more bandwidth you can create in your communication lines.

As a bonus, once you are skilled at using it, it keeps working over email, chat and so on.

17 Change your mind: your product is your team - Jose Ramón Diaz

The following is a guest post by Jose Ramón Díaz[a]. Jose :I have been developing software for more than ten years, and now I try to share agile principles and practices as the best way to improve organizations and teams. I am interested in promoting the teams to become effective and efficient, while also enjoying their work. I try to do my best as an agile coach.

[a]http://najaraba.blogspot.com/

You should change your mind about what you are building when you become project manager or team leader (as a boss). Forget your product. Look at your team. Suddenly, you do not have to worry about technical decisions or pretty interfaces. You must realize that the basics of your work has changed. My own inspiration is the mantra "team = product".

The product will be as good as your team is. The behaviour of your team will determine the qualities of the product.

So, your product as project manager is the team. Invest in the team. This will change dramatically your efforts, now redirected to make the team to grow.

I first read that idea in the book "Software for your Head[1]", by Jim and Michelle McCarthy. This was annoying and shocking for me. But now I believe every little effort to improve your team is translated to the products they create. And you must be ready for that. Your behavior must change to let your people do their best. If you have been assigned as project manager recently, start studying again! (little advice: read, and read a lot!) You have no more technological related problems. I love Cockburn´s cite: "If you do NOT know anything about human behaviour, you know very little about software development". So, stop and think about your previous work, do you really know something about people and their behaviours?

Start changing your focus. From product to team. From technology to people.

Pay attention to people and identify the phase in which your team is and what it needs to evolve. Find the right leadership at the time, but admit you can not get to become the leader, but only that person who turns mediocre teams into great teams, a great manager.

If you keep thinking about building products, these will be only as good as you were able to create managing and controlling your team. However, if you facilitate the emergence of the full potential of your team, the product will be enhanced and enriched by many people and their synergies.

---

[1]http://tinyurl.com/leaderbooklink1

18 Leadership and the mature team by Mike Burrows

The following is a guest post by Mike Burrows[a]. Mike is a former global development manager and IT Director, now responsible for Kanban curriculum development at David J Anderson & Associates, Inc. His blog (positiveincline.com[b]) covers open source development and his recent Kanban implementation.

[a]http://twitter.com/asplake
[b]http://positiveincline.com

Roy's second chapter about the three team phases rings true to much of my experience as a team member, project leader, and development manager, but still it touches a red button of mine! I'm grateful to Roy for his very gracious offer to let me respond to it.

My red button? I worry about the Agile community's recent focus on self-management. Don't get me wrong: self-management is a good thing, but in its current popular usage it has two problems:

1. It fails to capture satisfactorily the much more powerful

concept (borrowed from the study of systems) of self-organization.

2. There seems to be a move in the community to minimize the role of leadership.

Self-organization is at the heart of agile methods, indeed it is the 11th of the 12 principles behind the Agile Manifesto. Definitions vary, but, in this context, it describes the ability of a system (here the project team) to create for itself ways to increase its own effectiveness.

Looking at the team from the outside, we see "emergence"â€"new behaviors arising without external intervention. In the Scrum context this might happen as a result of team retrospectives (the 12th principle) or simply through the individual contributions of team members. Either way, it's important to recognize that some of these new behaviors (i.e. innovations) may be highly non-standard.

Leadership (whether from within or without) takes the team to places it would otherwise never have reached, perhaps never even have considered. This can be in terms of the team's internal structures or its external goals, but, in the absence of leadership, it is a rare thing for a team to take itself out of its comfort zone, to redefine its approach to the outside world, perhaps even to completely reinvent itself.

Here's the paradox: good leadership encourages emergence, but the leader must also be ready to take the team out of the ecological niche it has carved out for itself, however, effectively. Yes, self-management is needed at every level (or the leader has time only for management), but we need also the humility to recognize its limits. Now, there is true maturity!

Mike Burrows
http://positiveincline.com http://twitter.com/asplake

19 Spread your workload - John Hill

The following is a guest post by John Hill[a]. JohnÂ is a .NET Team Leader / Senior Developer for a small Australian CMS software development company.

---

[a]http://www.foxhound.com.au/

During my many years of experience as a team lead (albeit only very recently in software development) I have seen other team leads "flog their workhorses". In many team environments, there will be members who are less likely to willingly accept tasks that they don't enjoy - the "complainers" (i.e. they kick up a stink) and those who just get their heads down and complete any task that you give them - the "reliables". I have seen many team leaders, including myself in my early years, naturally give the less fun jobs to the "reliables" as there is less chance of resistance and less chance of conflict with the person they're assigning the task to.

In the very short term, this strategy may work in your favour, however there are some repercussions:

1. The team as a whole may begin to pass work off to the "reliables".

2. The "reliables" will eventually burn out.
3. The "reliables" will become frustrated and you will more than likely lose their respect.
4. Internal conflict will arise as the "reliables" will separate themselves from the "complainers".

The solution involves sharing the load equally. If you gave a "boring" task to Member A today, give the "boring" task to Member B tomorrow - regardless of whether they complain. This will build up a culture of every team member being equal.

20 Making your team manage their own work - Lior Friedman

The following is a guest post by Lior Friedman[a]. About Lior: I'm an Agile coach and Software Craftsman with more than fifteen years of experience. In recent years I consult and train teams worldwide on how to improve software development. Specifically, I help companies adopt Agile software development processes and teach development teams how to improve the quality of their code by using advanced techniques like TDD, BDD and other Agile practices.

[a]http://imistaken.blogspot.com/

I was reading this post by John Hil[1] in the 5whys blog recently. and it got me thinking. I took me a while to understand why I felt that one is a little wrong. After all the advise given in it is quite reasonable. and then it hits me.

[1]http://5whys.com/blog/spread-your-workload.html

The game of picking who does what, is not worth playing.

It is better to avoid the problem to begin with, and the best way to do that is to let the team decide on its own who does what.

If you want to become a great team leader you need to stop being the team "task dispatcher". Normally a group of people will do a better job at this then a single person. Your jeb (as the team leader) is to allow this to happen. i.e. make your team self manage.

If your team is not yet there, here is a good goal for you to strive for and invest effort in. The first step is to stop deciding for them. As long as you decide who does what, the team will not take charge of its own work. After all why should they worry when you do this for them?

Now, I know this is not that simple to accomplish. but here's what works for me when I approach this problem.

Making your team manage their own work

Explain the new "rules" to the team – when expecting some- one to start doing something new, I found it usually helps to state my expectation. so the first thing is simply to tell them that from now on I expect them to divide the work between them (I also say that if they find it difficult I'm willing to help).

Teach them how to do it – When I ask for someone to do something new I like to make sure they know how to do it. In this case I would explain how I think tasks should be divided.

I give my tips and advises on how to balance the work, how to make sure everything is done as fast as possible and what I would expect to see.

I found that visualizing a problem goes a long way in solving it. and in this case I devise a way to put all the work "tasks" into a single visible place. I found that a physical task board does a very good job at this. so that's my preferred technique, but an excel list can do just as well.

As a lead, I do make sure to track how the team is doing (at least when at start). So a mechanism for tracking this should also be decided on. Again a Task Board does a great job at this, but a shared excel task list with the people names also works just as well.

And last, like any new skill, mistakes will be made along the way. That's ok. Mistakes are what people learn from, so don't try to prevent them, make sure the damage isn't too big, and that people learn from them.

21 Go see, ask why, show respect by Horia Slushanschi

About Horia: Horia is a passionate agile coach, serving as the leader of the HP Agile Mentoring Office and the HP Software Engineering Profession. He has written software of various kinds, from firmware for various devices, to compilers for supercomputers, and all sorts of business systems in between for more than 25 years now. Horia holds a PhD in Computer Science, is a trained Lean Six Sigma Black Belt practitioner, and holds various other certifications and memberships in various professional associations. His calling lies in growing more accomplished leaders, helping numerous teams to achieve amazing results.

The best way to help your team to serve their clients ever better, to achieve and sustain a culture of continuous improvement, is to start by showing them deep respect.

How can you best show respect? Consider Jim Womack's excellent advice in his collection of essays "Gemba Walks"[1].

---

[1] http://tinyurl.com/teamleaderbooklink2

You do so by challenging their thinking about the current work process, asking lots of open, probing questions to uncover the root causes of the current impediments. No process is ever perfect, so you can focus on helping the team to discover what its key constraint is at any particular time and then devise countermeasures to remedy it.

The key constraint is the area in which an improvement will show the biggest bang for the buck when measured across the entire system, improving the overall flow of the work process, likely reducing cycle time and waste, with less overburden or absurdity involved.

By engaging your team in problem-solving, you're showing them that you choose not to attempt to solve the problem alone. You trust them to be best placed to come up with the most promising improvement ideas, as they are closest to the work being done and have all the facts in hand. As a team leader, you truly respect your team's knowledge and their dedication to finding the best answer.

Even so, team members can't quite do it all alone because they are often too close to the issue to fully appreciate its full context. They may also avoid tough questions about the nature of the work and the reasoning behind certain inefficient practices. By showing mutual respect, better countermeasures can be devised, the team can derive more pride in the quality of their work, and everyone can enjoy a more satisfying journey of professional accomplishment.

To better serve your team, work to understand yourself better, assessing your own strengths and weaknesses. Strive to become aware of your team's characteristics as well, sensing their professional and emotional development needs. Be ready to adapt your leadership, coaching, and mentoring style to suit the team's current spot on its journey to professional mastery.

22 Keep Developers Happy, Reap High-Quality Work by Derek Slawson

About Derek: I'm a part of the software development team working for the physician group at one of Chicago's most prestigious medical institutions, Northwestern Memorial Hospital. I'm an unofficial team leader trying to advance our team forward during a unique situation–we're sort of a side project for our manager, who is now largely absent due to other responsibilities, and he has less and less time for us as the months go on (a scenario that is slowly being rectified). I was also the official manager of a small development team at a previous company though, admittedly, I've learned so much more about what a development team needs in my current managerless situation than I did in that prior position. I have a natural inclination towards best practices and learning new things, so I've tried to fill in the vacuum on our team as best as possible.

One of the most important lessons I've learned is that if you keep your developers happy and motivated, they'll end up doing some of their best work and will contribute to the betterment of the team and the organization. Some of the tricks involved with keeping them motivated, however, may initially seem to be counterintuitive to the developers and/or management.

First and foremost, you need an agreed-upon team coding standard, but then you can't neglect it. You need to thoroughly enforce it. While some developers may find that this gets nit-picky, it ultimately ensures that you have a codebase that follows the same standards and patterns throughout, which makes it much easier to maintain and train new staff on in the future. This also has the added benefit of enabling your developers to quickly turn out new code, since they aren't getting hung up on fixing bugs with an underlying framework or trying to decipher a monster 1000-line method. And, of course, being able to focus mostly on new applications or functionality keeps the developers feeling productive and fulfilled.

Another beneficial tactic to keep the team happy is to encourage the team to use a set time during the workweek to learn new skills or technologies (maybe just an hour, maybe as much as a day). Management will often initially scoff at this since they don't want to see valuable development time being spent on non-work. However, there are multiple benefits to be had from this, many of which will result in a better end product and, thus, happier management. Just being able to explore a new topic that interests the developer may be rewarding enough to keep them motivated to produce their best work. If it ends up being something that can benefit the entire team, though, the developer can present their findings to the others, and your end product may now improve too. Using new technologies often inspires developers, and management gets some new buzzwords to use in advertising the product.

One last motivational technique is another one that can make management cringe: *you absolutely need to establish that you prioritize quality over quantity.* When developers are encouraged to get projects done quickly, no matter what it takes, the end result is often incredibly sloppy coding and design, and you'll end up paying for it greatly later on down the line. Want to enhance your product and add new functionality a year later? Guess what–it's now going to take you several times as long to do so, since the spaghetti-like code may have made sense to the developer(s) working on it at the time, but it's almost guaranteed to require a great deal of study a year later in order to make sense of what it actually does, whether or not the original developers are even still on staff. Your team has to focus on untangling the code before they can even begin to write a single line towards a new feature. Focusing on quality upfront, at the cost of extra development time, almost certainly ensures that it will pay dividends and make it up several times over later on. The developers are motivated by producing quality work today that they are proud to stand behind, and they spend less mind-numbing time reworking a poor product in the future.

Overall, creating high standards for your team keeps your developers doing what most developers like doing best–creating new things. And when they're producing high-quality work and feeling happy, so is management!

23 Stop Doing Their Work by Brian Dishaw

About Brian: I am a leader who embraces failure and uses experiences to empower, teach, and grow others.

Chances are you got put into a leadership position because you were good at your previous job. Continuing this behavior as the leader, however, is a dereliction of your current responsibilities. In other words, this means you aren't focusing on learning and growing in your current position. In addition, you are taking away opportunities for your team to learn and grow in their positions. Worst of all, you are actively building a team that has an absence of trust, a lack of accountability, and low commitment to what they are doing.

I was promoted to a lead developer of on a team of which I was a developer from day one. I helped build the system from the ground up and had very intimate knowledge of its more complicated and critical subsystems. This worked really well when my job was to build the system.

It was very quick for me to identify what needed to happen. I had the history of the way it was built (within reach if not with in my head), so deciding direction and impact came without too much effort. We then started to grow the team of four to a team of 30 (over a year or so) and then, shortly after, I was promoted.

Soon enough, things grinded to a halt. I found myself wondering why as I ran off and put out fire and after fire by "cleaning up" after my developers. Retrospective after retrospective, the team would push back by saying things like, "Brian is never around," "Brian is too busy to help me, so it's taking me longer than I expected to complete this work," and "Brian is always in meetings."

It didn't take long for the situation to further decay because my reaction to what they were saying was wrong because I took it literally. I was around more and very visible where I was when I had to be gone. I was saying to people that I trusted what they were building (only to have to swoop in and clean up something later). The quality of the product deteriorated quickly and velocity was virtually glacial. I never did manage to help the team with their real problems with ownership, accountability, and trust. I didn't even *realize* what I had done to that team until roughly six months after leaving that team for a different one within the same company.

I can reflect now that what they were saying was not "Brian is never around," or "Brian is always in meetings." It was "Brian doesn't trust us so I need to make sure I get his sign-off before I continue."

That one statement sums up thre of the major dysfunctions of a team:

- Absence of trust

- A lacking of accountability
- Low commitment to what they are building

I did that to them not because I didn't trust them or that I didn't want them to be successful. It was because I took their growth opportunities from them. I was also failing to learn how to be an effective leader. The worst part is that I was once the catalyst for a healthy velocity of the product only to turn around and make it grind to a halt. If I had realized then what I know now, things could've been better for that team. It still would have been difficult to let go, but every time I slipped I would have had something to fall back so that I could try again.

24 Write code, but not too much by Patrick Kua

About Patrick: Patrick Kua works as an active, generalising specialist for ThoughtWorks and dislikes being put into a box. Patrick is often found leading technical teams, frequently coaching people and organisations in lean and agile methods, and sometimes facilitating situations beyond adversity. Patrick is fascinated by elements of learning and continuous improvement, always helping others to develop enthusiasm for these same elements. You can find out more about him at http://www.thekua.com/atwork/

I've worked with many team leaders, and one of the most difficult activities is balancing time spent writing code versus other leadership activities. In an extreme case, writing no code leads to a lack of specific context for any strong directions you might push the team. Even with the most positive of intents, without grounding in a system's current state, any decisions you make might cause more work than needed. In the other extreme case, writing too much code probably means other important leadership activities are being neglected and any broader technical issues remain unresolved.

Other circumstances often dictate the time you have to code. Your leadership role means representation in many more meetings. Time in meetings will pull you away from writing code. You will also find some of these meetings much more ad hoc, making any coding effort difficult to do so without interruption.

I've found that accommodating and balancing a team leader's need to code is easiest in teams practicing pair programming as long as there also practise frequent rotation and collective code ownership. The idea is that you can help work with your pair to design a solution, or at least, agree on a direction to take for solving a problem. If you find yourself dragged off to meetings, then any functionality being built or changed does not stop being developed, and you can rejoin with only a slight interruption to progress. Your team still benefits from you having specific knowledge about the codebase, balancing out the other activities your role requires you to do.

For teams who don't practice pair programming, any coding time you find is best spent on tasks away from the critical path, particularly if it's likely to block others from completing their work. For some people, this might be a scary idea but you need to have trust in the team or least ensure that the team has the right mix of skills to tackle critical issues. Great team leaders delegate tasks early, combining frequent design or code reviews to ensure overall standards are met.

Other coding activities team leaders should strive for are looking for critical technical debt that serves to continually drag at the team, looking at ways of breaking down larger chunks into smaller, manageable chunks. As tempting as it might be for team leaders to take all the "interesting stuff," teams succeed best when their leaders help them remove impediments and let the team work out the best way to get stuff done.

25 Evolving from Manager to Leader by Tricia Broderick

About Tricia: Tricia Broderick is one of the directors of development at TechSmith, which builds innovative tools Snagit, Camtasia Studio, Camtasia Relay, Coach's Eye, Jing, and Screencast.com to facilitate visual communication. Tricia is responsible for creating and maintaining an engaging and empowering environment for software engineering teams to deliver high quality products. With sixteen years of experience, the last six of which focused on agile principles, her passion for mentoring and coaching has been essential in successfully transitioning from a manager to an agile leader. Recently, her team summarized her leadership by highlighting that she knows just when to honestly challenge someone out of their comfort zone while continuously providing support and encouragement.

Dear Tricia of 2000,

This year seemed like the logical choice to select. Professionally, you have successfully managed several small projects and have received numerous recognitions. Personally, you just got engaged and most importantly, Michigan State University won the national basketball title! So your awesome mood coupled with your next assignment of managing your first thirty-person team should make you fairly receptive to this message.

Easily I can remember how much you pride yourself on being highly dependable. Yet, I know that as a manager you struggle with not feeling in control. Your solution is focusing towards hands-on risk mitigation. You will even convince yourself this is in everyone's best interest as the task needs to get done and you are simply setting an example, thus coaching others to avoid problems. The flaw in this logic will be missed for years as you'll have good success both in customer delivery and group dynamics. I can already hear you ask, "Exactly, where's the problem?. Are you really ok with results that are just good? Or do you want awesome results for yourself and your teams?" That's what I thought; just humor me and keep reading.

Being only a manager will produce good results. But evolving into a leader first that has the capability to manage will produce empowered teams that achieve awesome results. Don't even bother thinking it; not only are you are not a leader today, you won't be able to change something tomorrow and immediately become a leader.

Your evolution from a manager to a leader will be a primarily based on a combination of two assets. The first one is your ability to adapt and handle any risk or issue. Your high dependability was not a result of problems never occurring (as if!) but how you were able to effectively minimize impacts and leverage opportunities appropriately. The second one is your passion and skill for coaching and mentoring. And you've already experienced that people appreciate when you invest in helping them grow.

You're lucky—adapting and the desire to help others comes naturally to you. But there's a catch; to be aware and possess these assets will not be enough. You have other core traits that you often rely on that impact teams from being empowered. Specifically, you will need to lessen the desire for being the go-to expert and wanting perfection. For example, you've already learned that responding to a problem on the team with "I should just fix that myself" will not scale. However, you've only adjusted the response to, "What didn't I teach them to avoid this problem?", which means that you expected your team to be perfect through your help. Now don't go overanalyzing with a thousand examples of why they could have avoided a problem. There absolutely is a time and a place for coaching as this is the important capability to manage aspect. The problem is the leader mindset has to be first impulse, which requires a response of "How can I help them learn and adapt from this?." Your focus has to be in creating an environment that is dedicated to helping teams and individuals become adaptive, learning-focused, and cohesive.

There's no sugar coating the amount of work becoming a leader will take. You will have to maintain the skills necessary to have the capability to effectively manage. At the same time, begin with the work required to build trust both ways in order for people to be empowered. As this will be the easier part given your integrity and intentions are pretty visible and we all know you have no issues talking. The trick is in remembering that numerous situations are usually required before you will trust that they can adapt and more importantly, they fully believe that you trust them to adapt. Then tackle the challenging work that will drive you crazy;

embracing failure as a learning opportunity despite knowing it could have been prevented. You will have to constantly remember that your perspective should be on them; what's best for their growth even when you and/or they might look bad in the process.

I realize the devil's advocate in you is probably wondering whether all of this work is worth the difference in results. Without any hesitation, the answer is yes! You'll begin experiencing team results that exceed your even your highest expectations. You'll find yourself more engaged at work with the challenges that you now face. But the factor that really makes the answer so obvious is the satisfaction from helping others. The recognition you are receiving today pales in comparison to what you will experience as a leader. I still smile when I think about the time my team surprised me with an appreciation award. To hear numerous people stand up and highlight these types of statements: "I appreciate the way she pushes me out of my comfort zone in a way that makes me feel supported" to "I appreciate how she calls me out on my BS" all the way to "I appreciate her helping to pick out gifts for my wife." I couldn't help but walk out of that conference room proud of my team and, consequently, proud of myself too because I helped create an environment that I want to work and play hard in every day. That is worth everything!

Your future self, Tricia of 2013

26 Affecting the pace of change by Tom Howlett

About Tom: I've been developing web applications using Microsoft technologies for the last 15 years with a particular enthusiasm for Agile principles, Scrum, and Kanban. I've spent the last 5 years as a Scrum master and have enjoyed blogging about the experience on http://diaryofascrummaster.wordpress.com.

I'm in a lucky and rare position to have been with the same team for more than 10 years (more than half of the original team remain although we are all greatly 'changed'). In that time we've come from chaos to self organising, the team is happy and effective and constantly challenging the status quo. We are proud of what we achieved. I think our only regret is we didn't get there faster. Luckily you've got the wisdom in this book to help you achieve that.

So, 10 years is a long time, more time than most teams will get to become effective before they are outsourced. Why did it take so long? Agile development is all about shortening feedback loops. Perhaps if we had done this more aggressively, it may have helped, but, on the other hand, too much feedback too soon can be overwhelming, causing anxiety and building walls. The skill to facilitate change as a leader is to learn the techniques to help and encourage others to adopt change whilst remaining a happy and effective team.

Ideas for change should be coming from within the team as well as from you. They will come from reflection on what's not right and inspiration from what other teams are doing. Encourage the team to network at user groups, read blogs and use Twitter, and so on. These resources can make a huge difference to a team's enthusiasm for change.

For change to be adopted successfully, there needs to be consensus. As a team lead, it's your job to ensure there are opportunities to build consensus: retrospectives, stand-ups, or spontaneous chats are where it happens, so ensure that these happen when necessary and are environments for constructive dialogue. If you want to run these, well it is worth learning facilitation techniques from books like Jean Tabaka's *Collaboration Explained: Facilitation Skills for Collaborative Leaders*.

Your team will hopefully contain different personality types. Some will be focused on getting things done, some will be looking at the details, and some will be finding creative solutions to difficult problems. This will always cause tension. In the early days, the tension will create anxiety and frustration, but as you get better at collaborating, this tension will contribute to the effectiveness. The key to making this transition is to encourage the team to value each other's different strengths and understand that the strengths combined will help each member to become stronger.

If you are continually improving, there will be conflict. If there isn't, it's a good warning sign that you are stagnating. It is important to every team member that they are respected for being competent at their job. New ideas that challenge the way they currently work have the potential to challenge the feeling of competence leading to embarrassment. Our brains put up strong defences to avoid this from happening, particularly at first. Don't become frustrated by this; be sensitive, but don't let it stop you.

If a discussion starts going in circles with multiple people pushing their opinion and you can't see a way out, draw the meeting to a close, don't be despondent, and look and find out why. Take time to talk to people individually but ensure that you remain the person's equal in the conversation. Look at the work of Chris Argyris to ensure you get the most out of these conversations (check out the resources section on Benjamin Mitchell's blog http://blog.benjaminm.net/argyris/). Ask questions and try to ensure you are spending as much time enquiring into the cause of their issue as you are advocating yours. If it doesn't work, give it another day or two and talk again. In advocating your cause, explain the evidence that backs up the need to change and explain and question your assumptions. When trying to understand their point of view, try to find out the evidence and assumptions they have made to reach their conclusions. With practice, you can use these techniques within the original meeting.

Attempt to find a pace of change that's not causing too much anxiety on team members. Using the techniques above, it can be a much faster and smoother transition. Don't become disheartened; change takes time. Give others time but ensure you are helping the process as much as you can.

27 Proximity Management by Jurgen Appelo

About Jurgen: Since 2008 Jurgen writes a popular blog at www.noop.nl, which deals with development management, software engineering, business improvement, personal development, and complexity theory. He is the author of the book *Management 3.0: Leading Agile Developers, Developing Agile Leaders*, which describes the role of the manager in agile organizations. And he wrote the little book *How to Change the World*, which describes his new supermodel for change management.

When I just started as a manager, I had my own big office with a shiny desk, a new, fast computer, and a desk phone with more buttons than the ceremonial suit of an average dictator. I also had a workforce of a dozen software developers, to do with as I pleased. I lacked just one thing: I had no clue how to be a manager.

When I investigated my "communication issue," I realized its solution is based on proximity. Sitting side by side in the same room is more effective than having two people sit in private offices next to each other.

27.1 The first approach: move your ass

When you understand that distance reduces communication, you can try to optimize communication by optimizing proximity. The suggestions on *how* to do this differ in detail, but they all boil down to the same thing: the manager should move away from their desk, toward the work that is important to her. The advice is often presented under the Japanese name Gemba, which says the manager ought to be there where the work happens in order to understand how healthy the organization is and to help solve any problems people might have, using facts and not assumptions. Other names you may find are Genchi Genbutsu, *Go and See and Management by Walking Around (MBWA)*. And, in the case of distributed teams, this could become Management by Flying Around (MBFA).

27.2 The second approach: move your desk

Years ago, I realized that the concept of "being there where the work happens" can be taken a step further. I solved it by picking up my stuff to go sit with my team at a normal desk. This allowed me to pick up much more of what was going on. People spontaneously asked for my opinion and I picked up signs of joy and frustration, which I wouldn't have noticed if I had not been there.

When there are more teams involved, you can combine the two techniques according to two proximity principles:

1. Distance to people should match importance of work. So see what your teams are working on or how they work, and sit with the team that needs special attention.
2. Diversity in distance should match diversity of work. Optimize your communication with others by walking or flying around. There should be diversity in your distance to people, which depends on the diversity of their locations and their work.

Whatever you do, go to the problems. Don't wait for problems to find you.

28 Babel Fish by Gil Zilberfeld

About Gil: Gil Zilberfeld has been in software since childhood, starting out with Logo turtles. With almost 20 years of developing commercial software, he has vast experience in software methodology and practices. Gil is the product manager at Typemock, working as part of an agile team in an agile company, creating tools for agile developers. He promotes unit testing and other design practices, down-to-earth agile methods, and some incredibly cool tools. He speaks in local and international venues about unit testing, TDD, and agile practices and communication. And in his spare time he shoots zombies, for fun. Gil blogs at http://www.gilzilberfeld.com on different agile topics, including processes, communication and unit testing.

I don't remember much from my first day as a team leader. It could be because I was so entranced with being anointed with a title someone else has left behind. Or, maybe because it was so many years ago.

Since then, I've learned many things about what I should have done on that fateful day instead, and in the following years. I didn't realize it then but on that day I became a Babel Fish.

(If you don't know, a fictitious animal, in Douglas Adams' books, which performs instant translations [Wikipedia].) That wasn't on-the-job description. Still, as a new team leader, communication and translation of information is the most crucial role you now have, and from now on, your task is to improve as one.

28.1 A team leader needs to communicate in multiple channels

Up, down, and sideways. Information about business require-ments and needs, risk, and stability issues, you name it. Let's take the first example, a new business requirement was just added to the project. Your team can work off a spec, but it work out better if you can communicate correctly the motivation behind that requirement, in a language that the team can understand. Or, let's say the team identified a risk when implementing the requirement. You can just update the status to, "We'll be late by 2 weeks, sorry." It would be more effective, though, to communicate the reason behind the delay, in a language that the business people can understand. Most people don't even understand that others don't speak their language. Team leaders provide translation services, so everyone will head in the right direction. That's you, buddy!

Awareness is the first step. The next step is harder: To become a successful Babel Fish, you need to learn more languages than you already know. That's business language, technical language, tester language, marketing language, sales lan-guage, HR language. In order to do that, you need to go out, converse and learn.

Get out of the development silo and start talking to other humans. It ain't easy, but it's worth it.

Apart from your team benefiting from better information, including the "why do this" factor, you get a bonus: better relationship with people from other departments. You'll need it in order to improve your team. Imagine what it would be like if the HR guy would let you skip filling a few forms, when you just had interviewed a star you don't want to miss out on? You can benefit your team even from the outside, by having trust relationship with everyone else. If you make this your priority, everything else will fall in line. To better communicate with your team, you'll need to talk with them more. This way, you'll know how to improve their effectiveness and challenge them with the tasks that befit them. Your team will get respected because they finally have a team leader that normal people can talk with. It's like relationship inheritance, if you think about it. Most of all, you'll grow as a person, as a team leader, and as a communicator. As everyone knows, it's all about communication.

Congratulations on your new job, Babel Fish!

29 You are the Lead, Not the Know-It-All by Johanna Rothman

About Johanna: Johanna Rothman, known as the "Pragmatic Manager," helps organizational leaders see problems and risks in their product development. She helps them recognize potential risks, seize opportunities, and remove impediments. She is the author of several management and project management books. You can read more about Johanna and find her blogs and her writings at http://www.jrothman.com

One of the traps that team leads encounter is the trap of having to know it all. It doesn't matter if you're team lead of three people or thirty people. You got to be a team lead because of your technical skill, right? That must mean you're pretty smart, and you're supposed to lead, right? You're supposed to have lots of great ideas. You're supposed to know lots of things. You're supposed to be able to solve lots of problems. Well, that doesn't mean you have to solve every problem yourself.

Many years ago, when I was a technical lead, I was also the project manager. We were a three-person project. I was the team lead, Andy was my junior person, and Mark was my mechanical engineer. We were working on a machine vision project back in the mid-1980s, when cameras were able to collect up to eight bits of data per pixel. (That's not megabits; that's just eight bits.)

Andy and I were working on the software for gauge inspection. Mark helped us by creating the gauge holder. Yes, it took three of us to implement this project. The gauges were similar to the gas gauges or mileage gauges in your car back in the 80s; they were orange lines against black backgrounds with other white markings at regular intervals. Our job was to detect the angle of the orange line on the gauge.

With today's cameras, this is not such a difficult problem. With the cameras of 1984, the problem was huge. We needed to light the gauge just so. We needed to know if we were picking up the orange line, not the white markings. With only 8 bits per pixel, and the computing power back in 1984, you can imagine our problems.

I'd started developing the algorithms and asked Andy to continue. But the calculations were not 100 percent reliable. We were doing a code review when Mark came in to ask a question about the gauge holder. He listened for a minute. He asked some questions and soon we were all discussing whether the gauge holder should hold the gauges sideways or straight up.

I no longer remember the resolution to that problem. What I do remember is the power of the discussion. When I relinquished the power of being the *only* technical lead, everyone's problem-solving skills came to the fore. Everyone engaged in solving the problem. Everyone was more excited.

We did finish that project successfully. I suspect Andy's solution won, which is why I no longer remember. But that's the value of technical leadership–to facilitate the team to the best solution, not just your solution.

Did I know it all? No. Did I know enough? Yes. I knew enough to start problem solving and facilitate the rest of the team, finally.

Team leadership is not about knowing everything and doling out information and problem solutions. Team leadership is about creating an environment in which everyone can flourish to the best of each person's ability–including yours.

Loosen the reins on your team. You, too, will grow and flourish. That's the lesson I learned.

30 Actions speak louder than words by Dan North

About Dan North: Dan is an independent technology consultant who writes software and coaches teams and organisations in Agile and Lean methods. He believes in putting people first and writing simple, pragmatic software.

The way you act says more about your values than any pithy motivational slogan. A team is more likely to follow your lead in terms of your behaviour than they are to follow your instructions, especially if these aren't aligned. If you talk about valuing feedback and then get defensive when someone offers some, the team will unconsciously pick up on the defensive behaviour. Conversely if you always take the time to check in with your team, they will get into the habit of telling you things and may even become more comfortable talking with one another. Sometimes, this modelling can have a surprising upside, when you notice the team picking up a behaviour that is so intrinsic to your values you never even thought to make it explicit.

One of the toughest starts I had as a software team leader

involved joining a team of nine strongly-opinionated developers as their lead. They had formed cliques within the
team, and each thought the others were idiots and simply
didn't understand software. I was brought in primarily as an
unblocker: an external person who wasn't vested in any of
the cliques and who might be able to help them find a way
forward.

My first priority was to take each member of the team out for
coffee, one at a time, away from the office, and just listen. I
asked each person the same questions: what they liked and
what frustrated them about the team, the software and the
project, and what they wanted to change. The thing that
surprised me most was that they all saw the same issues and
wanted to make almost the same changes. Just before I got
there, the team had decided to introduce a design change
to make part of the code more understandable and were
busy arguing about how to implement it. There were some
differences in the details, and it was here that cliques were
forming. It seemed to me this was more about jostling for
position than about an objectively better or worse technical
solution.

I used a Shackleton[1] technique of asking everyone for their
input and then making a decision, while actively engaging
with and listening to dissenters. We went ahead with one of
the options and, after a couple of weeks, we realised it really
wasn't helping, and in fact the whole approach was making
things worse! I took the responsibility for a bad decision and
we backed out the change, cleaning up as we went. And
then a strange thing happened: people started to become
less defensive and even began experimenting a little. I had
inadvertently demonstrated that it was OK to try something
and fail, which unlocked a whole new style of working.